Productivity Kit

Adobe Press

San Jose, California

Productivity Kit

Adobe Press
San Jose, California

Contents

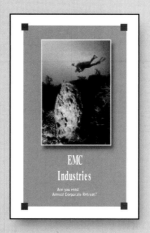

Introduction

The *Adobe® PageMaker® 6.5 Plus Productivity Kit* provides ideas, techniques, templates, and tips to help you get the most out of Adobe PageMaker 6.5 Plus.

The PageMaker 6.5 Plus CD-ROM supplies templates for all your business publication needs. In addition, the CD includes all the fonts used in the templates and hundreds of pieces of clip art and photographic images for you to use in customizing the templates.

By simply replacing the placeholder text with your own text and replacing the placeholder art with the CD art or your own art, logos, and scanned photographs, you can produce professional publications right on your desktop.

Using other Adobe software products

Several of the projects contain variations and tips for use with Adobe Photoshop® 5.0 Limited Edition LE and Adobe Acrobat® 4.0. For your convenience, a complete version of Photoshop 5.0 LE, the Acrobat 4.0 Reader and Acrobat 4.0 Distiller® software is included on the CD-ROM. For information on upgrading to the full versions of Photoshop 5.0 or Acrobat 4.0, see the Adobe Web site.

Using the projects

This book contains step-by-step instructions and design tips for a variety of projects—from creating simple business cards and black-and-white labels to producing full-color newsletters, brochures, posters, direct mail pieces, and annual reports. Many projects include variations to help you customize your work. Although each project highlights one template, the instructions can be used as a guide to working in any of the templates in that category.

To begin, follow the instructions in "Using the Templates" to learn some basic PageMaker 6.5 Plus skills and terminology. Then proceed to any of the projects to create the publications of your choice. Because each project provides stand-alone instructions, there's no need to complete the projects in the order that they appear in the book. Just pick the project that meets your needs, and prepare to be productive!

Tools:

Adobe PageMaker Plus

Templates:

Brochures 0000328

Fonts:

Bodoni

Using the Templates

Start here to learn how to get the most out of the PageMaker 6.5 Plus Productivity Kit templates.

Research shows that in less than five years, over 80% of purchases will be made using the computer. Will you company be ready to take advantage of this explosive marketing opportunity?

The World of E-Commerce is here to help! Now is the time to develop and implement your online marketing strategies. From analyzing your audience to designing your web site— we're have what you need.

With WOE you maintain control over your products and services. You decide what, how, and when you want to advertise. We handle the nuts and bolts of getting you (and keeping you) up and running on the Internet.

World of E-Commerce!

1234 Bridge Street
Twin Rivers, NY 01234
Phone: (555) 555-1111
Fax: (555) 555-1112

One of the main reasons given for not making purchases over the Internet is the issue of credit card fraud. Your customers don't need to worry about security when they order with WEC. We use the latest in encryption and secure server technology to assure that all information is kept strictly confidential.

Welcome to the World of E-Commerce!

Join the online revolution!

WEC provides an award-winning staff for you online business. Each is a specialist in their field of design, marketing, shipping and accounting. Orders sent to your site are shipped within 24 hours. You receive monthly reports of your web site activity. You're free to concentrate on what you do best—provide the best products at the best price.

World of E-Commerce!

Before you begin modifying the Adobe PageMaker Plus templates, take a few minutes to acquaint yourself with some of the tasks that are common to all the templates. Once you've mastered these basics, you're ready to jump into any of the projects.

Opening templates

PageMaker Plus includes over 300 professionally designed templates. When you open a template, PageMaker Plus automatically opens an untitled copy of the document. Because you're working in a copy, you never need to worry about altering the original template.

The templates are named with numbers, such as 2000465. When the template name begins with a 0 or a 1, it's a beginning template. Templates that start with 2 are intermediate templates, and those that start with 3 are advanced templates.

The way you open a template differs slightly depending on the kind of computer you're using.

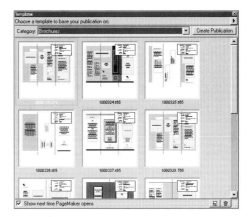

Windows. When you start PageMaker Plus in Windows, the Template palette appears. (If you don't see the palette, click the New Template button [🗋] in the toolbar).

To open a working copy of the template, choose a category from the menu at the top of the palette and then double-click the thumbnail of the template you want to open. In this example, we chose the Brochures category and opened template 0000328.

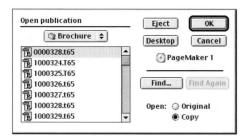

Mac OS. To open a working copy of a template in the Mac OS, insert the PageMaker 1 CD in your drive, start PageMaker Plus, and choose File > Open.

Navigate to the PageMaker CD and open the Templates folder. Open either the US Letter or A4 folders (depending on the paper size you're using), then open a category folder. Select the individual template and click Open. In this example, we opened the US Letter and Brochure folders, and selected template 0000328.

Installing fonts for templates

Although many of the fonts used in the PageMaker Plus templates are installed when you install the program, some are not. If a template requires a font that's not in your system, you'll get a dialog box when you open the template that tells you which fonts are missing.

You can easily install these fonts as you need them. The fonts are located in the Template Fonts folder on the PageMaker 1 CD. They must be moved into your system before they are available for the templates.

The information box (see page 6) for each template lists the fonts used in the template. The Materials section on the first page of each project also lists the fonts.

If you know you want to use a template, you need to load its fonts before you begin working in it. You can browse templates without having fonts installed by temporarily substituting other fonts (click OK when you see the Font Matching Results dialog box). If, after browsing, you decide you want to use a template, don't forget to add the fonts before you begin customizing the template.

The way you add fonts differs slightly depending on the kind of computer you're using.

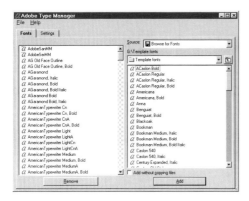

Windows. Choose Start > Program > Adobe > Adobe Type Manager® and click the Fonts tab in the (ATM) window. Navigate to the Template Fonts folder on the PageMaker 1 CD and select the fonts you want to load from the right column. Click Add. When the fonts you need for the template are installed, quit Adobe Type Manager.

Mac OS. Quit PageMaker Plus and open the Template Fonts folder on the PageMaker 1 CD. Drag the fonts you need to the Fonts folder inside the System folder, then restart your computer.

Note: If you're using ATM Deluxe® for the Mac OS, refer to the ATM Deluxe documentation for instructions on moving the fonts to your system.

Saving templates

After opening a template, save the copy on your hard disk and give it a name you can easily remember. To save a template, click the Save button (🖫) in the toolbar (Windows) or choose File > Save As (Mac OS).

Getting information about a template

Every template has a box in its upper right corner that provides information about the template, including its name, code, description, font family, production notes, output notes, and level of difficulty. To read this information, zoom in on the box.

Replace these gray boxes with your own photographs. If the photographs are in color, you might want to change the color of the background boxes to "pick up" a color in the photos. For instance, if the photo has a plum color in it, you might want to change the green boxes to something more plum-ish.

Beginning templates (those whose names start with a 0) also have design tips. These helpful suggestions not only provide tips for working with a particular template, they also describe general design tips and techniques.

After you've read the template information and the tips, you can hide them so they don't interfere with your work area. The information box and all the tips are on a single layer. To hide this layer, choose Window > Show Layers. In the Tips layer, click the eye icon in the far left column to hide the layer.

Locating images and clip art

All of the templates provide placeholders for text and art. You can replace these placeholders with your own art or you can choose from the images and clip art that comes with PageMaker Plus. The way you browse the art differs slightly depending on which kind of computer you're using.

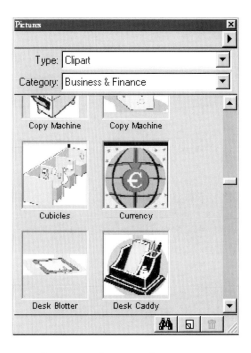

Windows. To browse the art in Windows, go to the Pictures palette (if it's not showing, click the Pictures palette button [⬚] in the toolbar). Choose a type from the Type menu. (All types displays both images and clip art.) Choose a category from the Category menu. PageMaker Plus provides more than 20 categories of art. Use the scroll bar and scroll buttons to see all the art in a category. Note the name of the art you want to use.

Mac OS. To browse the art on the Mac OS, insert the PageMaker 2 CD in your drive. Open the CD and double-click the Catalog.pdf file. The Adobe Acrobat 4.0 Reader opens so you can browse through the art. Click a category along the left side of the page. Use the forward and backward arrows to move through each category. Note the number of the art file you want to use.

In this example, we're locating the Currency clip art file (0003744.ai) from the Business and Finance category.

Deleting art placeholders

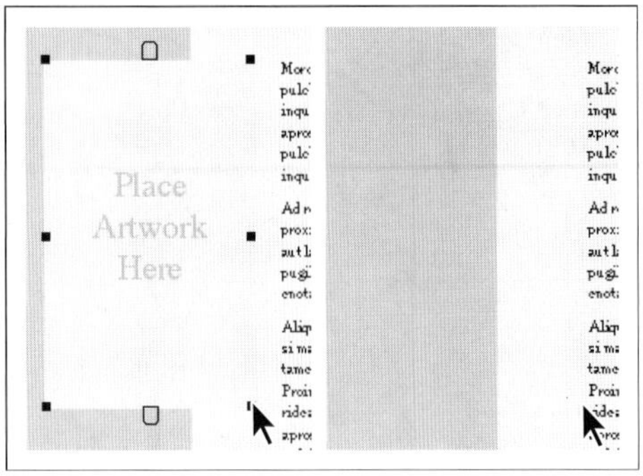

The easiest way to add art to a template is to delete an art placeholder and replace it with your own art or art from the CD. To delete a placeholder, use the pointer (↖) to select the placeholder, then press the Backspace (Windows) or Delete (Mac OS) key.

Adding art to templates

The way you add art to a template differs slightly depending on the kind of computer you're using.

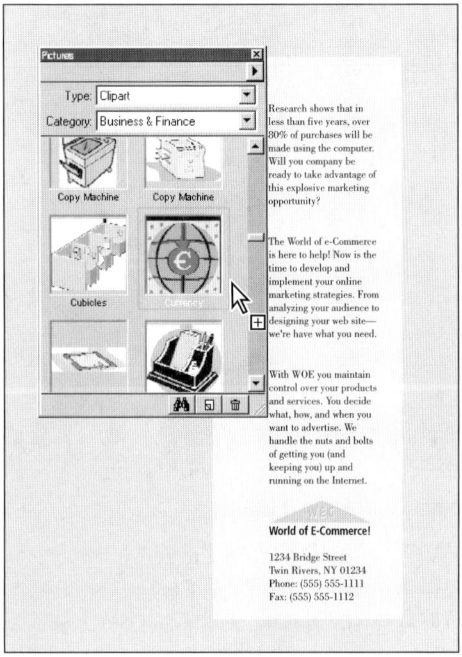

Windows. To add art in Windows, click the thumbnail in the Pictures palette (a yellow box appears around the thumbnail to tell you it's selected). Drag the thumbnail into the template window and move it into its final position.

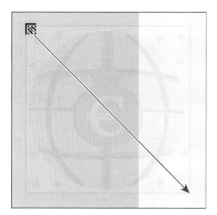

Mac OS. To add art to the template in the Mac OS, first locate the art and note its file name. Make sure the PageMaker 2 CD is in your drive and choose File > Place. Navigate to the CD and open the Library folder. Open the appropriate category folder and double-click the art file you want to use.

When you return to the template, the cursor appears with a PS inside of it (). To place the art, position the cursor where you want the upper left corner of the art to be, then drag. Use the pointer to move the art to its final position.

In this example, we deleted the art placeholder at the top of the middle panel and added the Currency (0003744.ai) clip art file in its place. We then deleted the logo placeholder at the bottom of the middle panel and added our own logo.

Resizing art

In many cases, the art you add to a template will be the correct size. There may be times, however, when you need to resize the art.

You can use two kinds of art in a PageMaker Plus template—vector graphics and bitmap images.

Vector graphics are created in a drawing program, such as Adobe Illustrator®. Because vector graphics are defined by mathematical objects, they can be resized, either up or down, without losing their sharpness. The clip art files supplied with PageMaker Plus (those with an .ai extension) are vector graphics.

Bitmap images, such as photos you scan and bring into PageMaker Plus, are made up of small squares known as *pixels.* Pixels are good at reproducing the subtle shading found in continuous-tone images.

Because bitmap images contain a fixed number of pixels, enlarging a bitmap image requires PageMaker Plus to spread out the pixels in the placed image to fit the larger size. The result can be a blurred image with loss of detail. You can decrease the size of bitmap images without any problems, but avoid increasing image size in PageMaker Plus. The image files supplied with PageMaker Plus (those with a .jpg extension) are bitmap images.

If you're going to have your publication professionally printed, talk to your printer about the images you're using. The printer may be able to resize the images for you.

Placing art in a frame

Instead of deleting a placeholder, you can choose to use its outline as a container for your art. When you select a placeholder, black handles appear around the edge of the frame. Placing your art inside a frame keeps the spacing consistent in the template.

In this example, we're going to place an image in the art placeholder in the left panel.

First, locate the image you want to use:

• In Windows, when you're placing art in a frame, you cannot drag from the Pictures palette. Instead, you use the Place command and select the art by its filename. To find the filename for a piece of art, select the art in the Pictures palette and choose Picture Properties from the Pictures menu. The filename appears at the end of the first line of identifying text.

• In the Mac OS, the art is identified by its filename. To locate the image, follow the instructions on page 6.

In this example, we placed the Credit Card image (0004761.jpg) from the Business and Finance catalog.

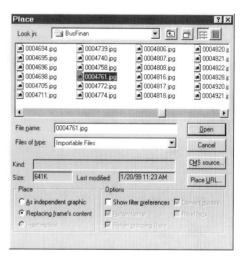

To place the art, click the Place button (⊞) in the toolbar (Windows) or choose File > Place (Mac OS), then navigate to the category folder and select the file. Be sure the Replacing Frame Content's option is selected in the Place dialog box and click Open. The art appears in the frame, replacing the gray box.

Repositioning and resizing art in a frame

When you place art in a frame, it is sometimes too large or the wrong section of the image is visible in the frame. You can easily change the position or size of the art.

One of the main reasons

To reposition art that is larger than a frame, select the crop tool (⌗) and drag. The image moves, but the frame stays in place.

If your art is smaller than the frame, you can select and resize the frame. For more on matching art and frame size, see Project 1.

To resize art in a frame, choose Element > Frame > Separate Contents. The art appears in full size on top of the frame. Use the pointer (⬉) and drag a handle to resize (press Shift as you drag to keep the image's proportions). When it's the right size, hold down Shift and select the frame *and* the art. Choose Elements > Frame > Attach Contents to put the art back inside the frame.

Replacing text

Every template has placeholders for text. These placeholders are filled with sample text to give you an idea of the fonts, styles, and text sizes used in the template.

Placeholder text appears in frames. To replace the text, select the existing text and begin typing. Because it's in a frame, the box for the text remains the same size, no matter how little or how much text you enter.

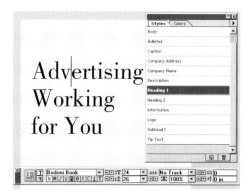

The text styles are listed in the Styles palette. To display the Styles palette, choose Window > Show Styles.

To identify the text style, select the text tool (**T**) and place the insertion point in the text. The style is highlighted in the Styles palette, and the text characteristics appear in the Control palette. For example, placing the insertion point in the large text in the right panel indicates that the text is in the Heading 1 style, which uses the Bodoni font in the 24 point size with 26 point leading (leading is the vertical space between lines of type).

The text in the middle column is in the Information style, and the text in the left panel is in the Description style.

In this example, we used the text tool to select the headline and entered new text.

Changing text styles

Because the text you enter may be longer or shorter than the sample text, or require different emphasis, you might want to change a text style. In this example, we modified the Heading 1 style.

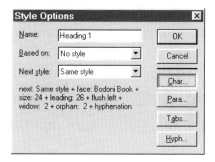

To edit a style, double-click the style in the Styles palette. The Style Options dialog box appears. You can change four style settings—paragraph, character, tabs, or hyphenation. In this example, we clicked the Char button to change the character settings.

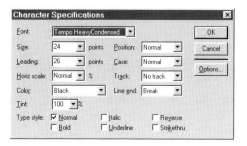

In the Character Specifications dialog box, we changed the font to Tempo Heavy Condensed. We left the size at 24 and the leading at 26.

Changing template colors

Every PageMaker Plus template has its own set of colors, which are listed in the Colors palette. To display the Colors palette, choose Window > Show Colors. You use this palette to modify or add colors to the template

Most of the templates use colors from the Pantone color system. This template, for example, uses a Pantone green and a Pantone mustard color, along with black and the paper color.

Along the top of the Colors palette are three boxes. When clicked, these boxes let you pick colors for the stroke (✎)(or outline) of objects, the fill (□), or both the stroke and the fill (▣) at the same time. Next to these boxes is the tint menu, which lets you choose color variations by changing their opacity.

To modify a color, select the object or text you want to change and click a new color in the Colors palette. For a less dramatic color change, choose a new tint. In this template, the background color is green at a 75% tint. We changed the tint to 100% for a bolder look. To emphasize the headline, we changed it to the mustard color and increased its tint to 100%.

There will be times when you will want to apply a completely new color scheme; for example, you may want to incorporate your logo colors in a design or create a brighter or more subdued effect for a specific publication. In addition to modifying the existing template colors, you can also add new colors to the Colors palette. For more information on adding new colors, see Project 17.

Printing templates

You have several options when it comes to printing the PageMaker Plus templates. For small jobs, such as signs, posters, and labels, you'll probably print on your desktop inkjet printer. For longer or more involved projects, or those requiring high print quality, such as business sets, brochures, and invitations, you'll probably bring your job to a quick-print center or professional print shop.

Template Type:	Brochure, Tri-Panel
Code:	0000328.T65
Description:	4 Color Process, suitable for color photography, no bleed
Font Families:	Bodoni
Production Notes:	Ensure that all photography is of adequate resolution for any offset printing requirements
Avery SKU #:	None
Technical Level:	■□□

The information box (see page 6) contains a Description line, which details the printing requirements for the template. This includes the number of colors, whether they are process or spot colors, Avery SKU numbers, and suggestions about the art in the template. (For more about Avery stock, see page 29. For more about spot colors, see Project 20. For more about process colors, see Project 24.)

If you plan to print the template on your desktop printer, it doesn't really matter how many or what types of colors are used.

If you're going to have the template printed by someone else, you need to keep a few things in mind:

• When you specify spot colors, the printer uses a different can of ink for each color in the template. The more colors, the more expensive the printing is. If the template uses black plus two other colors, it will cost even more.

• When you specify CMYK or process colors, you can have as many colors as you want. Process colors are printed using four separate color separations — cyan, magenta, yellow, and black. If you're going to use high-end, four-color printing, be sure to talk to your printing professional about requirements before you take in your job.

• Templates that call for bleeds (where color goes off the edge of the page) will not print well on your desktop printer, because desktop printers cannot print all the way to the edge of a page. When you want a bleed, talk to your printing professional before you create your PageMaker Plus file. Bleeds can often add to the cost of a print job.

When you're taking your output somewhere else to be printed, whether it's to a quick-print shop for added color or color copies or to a printer for output on a high-resolution image-setter, always talk to the print shop first. It can often offer suggestions and recommendations on ways to prepare your file that will save you time, trouble, and money.

Tools:

Adobe PageMaker Plus

Templates:

Flyers 1000529

Fonts:

Birch and AGaramond

Project 1

Illustrating Flyers with Clip Art

Use frame and drawing tools to illustrate your publications.

When you're adding art to a template, you're not limited to ready-made images or scanned photos. You can create original art for the publication using the PageMaker Plus drawing tools. You can even turn the drawings into frames.

There are three different ways to fit art into a frame—you can clip the art to fit the frame, you can scale the art to fit the frame, or you can resize the frame to fit the art.

① **Getting started.** Open Flyers template 1000529. Save the template with a new name and turn off the Tips layer.

Replace the logo and text. Use the pointer (**⭠**) to select and delete the logo placeholder, then add your own logo. Use the text tool (**T**) to select and replace the text with your own text.

In this example, we replaced the multiple lines of text at the top of the flyer with a single line. We also deleted the spiral graphic and the text placeholder at the bottom of the flyer.

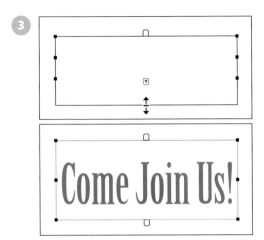

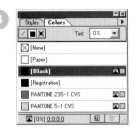

Style the text. When you enter your own text in frame, the current style sometimes needs adjusting. In this example, we applied the Headline style to the new text in the top frame. We also added emphasis to the first line of each paragraph by increasing the point size to14. For information on changing text styles, see page 13.

Sometimes when you apply a new style, the text disappears. This happens when the new style increases the point size, making the text too big to fit in the frame. Select the pointer and drag to increase the frame height to redisplay the text.

Remove the tint from the placeholder. Before placing art in a frame, it's a good idea to delete the gray tint. Then, if your new art doesn't fill the frame, you won't have leftover gray areas. Use the pointer to select the art placeholder, then change the fill tint to 0%. For more information about changing tints, see "Changing template colors" on page 14.

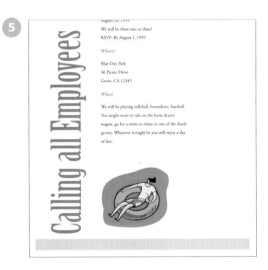

Place art in the frame. For more information about placing your art, see page 11. In this example, we placed the Inner Tube (0002258.ai) clip art file from the Recreation and Leisure category.

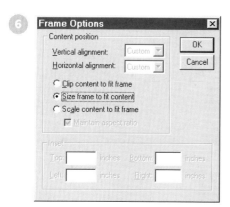

Fit the frame to the art. By default, PageMaker Plus clips the art to fit the frame. If your art is bigger or smaller than the frame, you can resize the frame to fit the art. Click the Frame Options button (⊡) in the toolbar (Windows) or choose Element > Frame > Frame Options (Mac OS). In the Frame Options dialog box, select Size Frame to Fit Content.

Instead of clipping the art or resizing the frame, you can scale the art to fit the frame. To scale the art, select Scale Content to Fit Frame in the Frame Options dialog box.

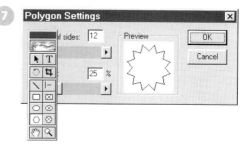

Select a drawing tool. To add original art to a template, use the PageMaker Plus drawing tools. Double-click a tool in the toolbox to set the tool options before you begin drawing.

To create the starburst, we used the polygon tool (○) with the number of sides set to 12 and the star insert set to 25% in the Polygon Settings dialog box.

Draw the shape. Drag the tool to add your shape. To draw the starburst, we dragged down and to the right. Holding down Shift as you draw constrains the starburst to a circle. (Make sure you draw your shape outside of a text column.)

Fill the shape with color. To fill a shape, select the shape with the pointer and click a color in the Colors palette. This starburst was filled with Pantone 5-1 CVS. For information on using the Colors palette, see "Changing template colors" on page 14.

Enjoy a
relaxing day
filled with fun
activities!

Add text to the shape. Select the text tool (**T**) and type to add text on top of the shape. To try out several looks, choose different fonts and sizes in the Control palette. When you're changing only a few lines of text, it's easier to choose options in the Control palette than to change the style using the Style Options dialog box (see page 13).

Save and print your flyer. Click the Save button (🖫) in the toolbar (Windows) or choose File > Save (Mac OS). A simple flyer like this prints well on a desktop printer.

Variation: Turn a shape into a frame

Experiment with other shapes using the rectangle and ellipse drawing tools. In addition to putting text into shapes, you can use shapes as art frames.

❶ Draw the shape and turn it into a frame. Double-click the tool to set the tool options, then draw a shape. Select the frame with the pointer and choose Element > Frame > Change to Frame. A large X appears inside the frame.

❷

Place the art. Choose File > Place and place your art (see page 11).

❸ Fit the art to the frame. To reposition the art in the frame, select the crop tool and drag. To fit the art to the frame, choose a content position in the Frame Options dialog box (see step 6 in the project).

As you begin to spread your design wings, you'll probably want to start experimenting with art. One easy way to expand the available art on the PageMaker Plus CD is to enlarge a piece of clip art and use that section as an individual piece of art.

To play with the clip art, choose File > New and open an empty publication. Drag or place the clip art in the publication, then drag the handles to resize. To keep the art's original proportions, hold down Shift as you drag. Because the clip art is a vector graphic (see "Resizing art" on page 10), you can make it as large as you want. Open a PageMaker Plus template and place the art in a frame. The frame will crop the art so that only a section of the enlarged art is visible. You can also enlarge the art while it's in a frame using the Element > Separate Contents command (see "Repositioning and resizing art in a frame" on page 12). When you reattach the contents to the frame, the art is cropped. You can't rotate the art and then reattach it. Instead, place the art in the frame and then rotate the frame.

For even more fun, try flipping the art using the horizontal-reflecting (F↔) or vertical-reflecting (F↕) buttons in the Control panel. For more on using these buttons, see Project 20.

Enlarged section of clip art placed in a frame

Clip art flipped using the horizontal-reflecting button

Clip art flipped using the vertical-reflecting button

Tools:
Adobe PageMaker Plus

Templates:
Business Cards 1000771

Fonts:
Orator

Project 2

Creating Instant Business Cards

Use guides to position elements and paste duplicates in a template.

The Business Card templates have multiple copies of the card on a single page. This duplication saves you time and money when it comes to printing the cards. The easiest way to complete these templates is to customize one card, delete the other card place-holders, and then paste new cards until the page is filled. This paste technique also works for other small item templates, such as labels and tickets.

Often, these multiple-on-a-page templates are designed to be printed on Avery stock. The business card stock, for example, has perforated edges so you can easily separate the individual cards. When a template layout is meant to be used on a particular Avery stock, the Avery SKU number appears in the template information box.

Getting started. Open Business Card template 1000771. Save the template with a new name and turn off the Tips layer.

Zoom in on one card. Click the Zoom tool (🔍) and drag around one card to magnify it.

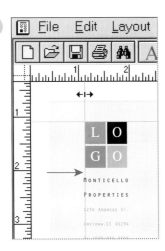

Add guides. The blue lines in a template are the nonprinting guides. (If the guides are not showing, choose View > Show Guides.) Guides help you line up the items in your layout. You can add guides anywhere on a page.

To add a horizontal guide, move the pointer over the horizontal ruler, hold down the mouse button, and drag a guide down to the top of the logo placeholder. Drag another horizontal guide and place it under the logo.

To add a vertical guide, move the pointer over the vertical ruler, hold down the mouse button, and drag a guide to the left edge of the logo. Drag a second vertical guide to the right edge of the logo. These guides serve to remind you of the original placement of the logo in the template.

Too many guides on a page can make it difficult to see the page. You can temporarily hide the guides by choosing View > Hide Guides.

To remove a guide, select it with the pointer and drag it off the page. To remove all the guides at once, choose View > Clear Ruler Guides. (If you have trouble removing a guide, choose View > Lock Guides. Guides must be unlocked before they can be deleted.)

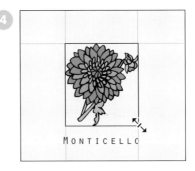

Replace the logo placeholder. Use the pointer (↖) to select and delete the logo placeholder and replace it with your logo. (For information on adding art to a template, see page 8).

If your logo is a different size or shape, resize it before you drag it into final position. Use the guides to place your logo as near as possible to the position of the logo placeholder. This example uses the Dahlias clip art (0005943.ai) from the Nature and Landscape category as its logo.

Replace the text. Use the text tool (**T**) to select and delete the card text. Enter your own text.

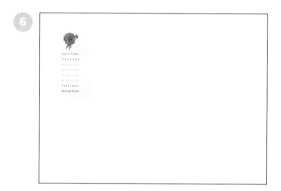

Delete the other cards. Choose View > Lock Guides to make sure the guides are locked in place. You don't want to move the guides inadvertently while you're deleting the other card placeholders in the template.

Select the pointer and hold down Shift as you select all the elements in the other card placeholders. Press the Backspace (Windows) or Delete (Mac OS) key.

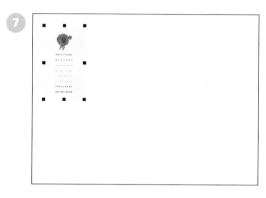

Group the objects. When you're copying and pasting multiple objects, it's easier to group them first. Grouping objects allows you to move them as a single unit. Shift-click to select the logo and the text frame. Choose Element > Group.

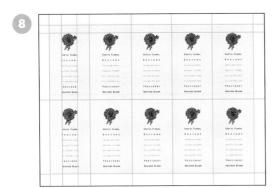

Copy and paste the group. Choose Edit > Copy. Zoom out so you can see more of the template, then choose Edit > Paste. Use the pointer to drag the card until it lines up with the guides. Continue to paste and position cards until you've filled the page.

Save the publication. Once you've filled the page with cards, save your file.

Print your cards. You can take your cards to a copy center or service bureau to have them printed, or you can print them on your own printer. See the input/output tip at the end of this project for information on printing cards on Avery stock.

Variation: Use a center guide

If your logo is not exactly the right width to match the width of the text frame on the template, you can resize the text frame. A single guide down or across the page works well when you're centering template elements.

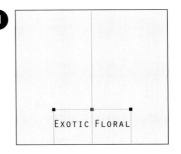

Create the guide. Since this is a vertical layout, you need to create a guide in the vertical center of the card. Drag a guide from the vertical ruler and place it in the center of the card.

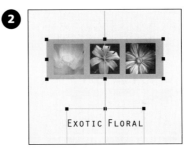

Place your logo. Add your logo and drag it above the text frame. Use the guide to center the logo over the text.

③

④

Resize the text frame. In this example, the logo is wider than the frame. Select the pointer (⬆) and click the text frame. Drag a handle to resize the text frame until it is the same width as the logo. Notice that the text keeps the same formatting but is expanded to fit the new width.

Center the text frame. Use the center guide to help you position the text frame.

Variation: Snapping to guides

By default, guides are set so that they exert a magnetic-like pull on any text or graphic within 3 pixels of the guide. This makes it easier to align text and graphics when the guide does not correspond exactly to a ruler marker.

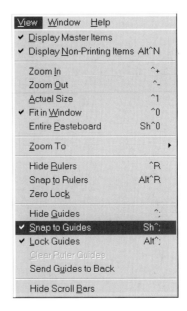

Turn off snapping. Select the grouped object and drag it close to a guide. Notice how the object snaps as it gets near the guide.

There may be times when you'll want to turn off snapping, for example, when you're trying to place art or text very precisely. Choose View > Snap to Guide to turn off this feature and try dragging the object again. To turn snapping back on, choose the command again.

Several of the PageMaker Plus templates are designed to be printed on Avery paper stock. Avery has a large supply of precut and prefolded papers that are perfect for business cards, self-seal mailers, labels, postcards, tickets, and so on.

Finding the Avery stock number

When the template will print well on an Avery paper, the Avery stock number (SKU) is included in the information box in the template's upper right corner.

Template Type:	Business Cards
Code:	1000771.T65
Description:	4 Color Process Business Cards
Font Families:	Orator
Production Notes:	None
Avery SKU #:	8371, 8372, 8376, 8377, 5371, 5372, 5376, 5377, **5911**
Technical Level:	■☐☐

Browsing the Avery catalog

Your print professional can show you the Avery catalog. You can also view the Avery catalog on line at www.avery.com.

It's a good idea to choose a stock before you create your publication. This is especially true if you'll be using a color stock or one with a design. Then you can use colors, fonts, and graphics that complement the paper.

Tools:
Adobe PageMaker Plus

Templates:
Tripak 2000748

Fonts:
Mac OS

Project 3

Adding Impact to Your Envelopes

Make your envelopes stand out with strong alignment and positive positioning statements.

EVER GREEN

123 A Street, Centerville, WA 01234
www.lawnservice.com
800 555 5555

Mrs. Virginia Brand
25 Buckelew Avenue
Centerville, WA 01234

"Friendly neighborhood lawn service for over 25 years"

FREE ESTIMAT

EVER GREEN

123 A Street, Centerville, WA 01234
www.lawnservice.com
800 555 5555

Mr. Rowlan
554 Spring Road
Geneva, OH 12345

Probably the most frequently seen advertisement for a small business is its envelope. Adding an unusual touch, such as a graphic or a positioning statement, personalizes and draws attention to your mailing. When you add new elements, you might need to adjust the overall alignment of the template. Remember to line up your edges and allow lots of white space to maintain a clear and crisp design.

Getting started. Open TriPak template 2000748. Save the template with a new name and turn off the Tips layer.

Replace the logo and text placeholders. Use the pointer (⬈) to select and delete the logo placeholder and replace it with your logo. Use the text tool (**T**) to select and delete the text. Enter your own company name and address information.

Add a positioning statement. A positioning statement tells your customers something that's special about your business. Like your logo and name, your positioning statement should appear on all your business pieces. Use the text tool to add a positioning statement to the envelope.

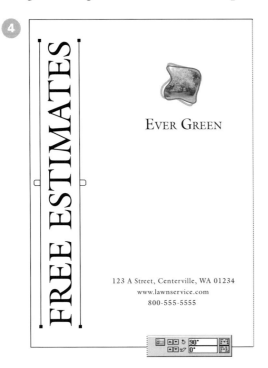

Rotate the text. We decided to run our positioning statement along the side of the envelope to be sure to grab our customers' attention. To rotate text, select the text frame with the pointer and type 90 in the Rotating option (↻) in the Control palette. Drag to position the text. We made the text fill the height of the envelope by adjusting the font size to 32 points.

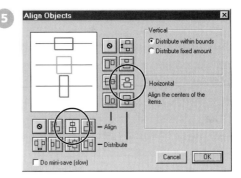

Align the objects. To balance out the strong line of text along the left edge, we wanted to space out the other envelope elements. Shift-click to select the objects you want to align (in this case the logo, company name, and address block). Choose Element > Align Objects (Windows) or Element > Align (Mac OS) and then select the alignment options. To space the elements, we chose the third from the top Distribute option. To center the objects, we chose the third from the left Align option. This centered, evenly spaced distribution reflects the center alignment of the text and presents a formal look.

Change the text alignment. For a more modern look, you can align all the elements to the right or left. To align text, use the text tool to select the text. Choose Type > Alignment and choose an alignment option from the menu. In this example, the text was aligned to the left in both text boxes.

Balance the layout. Make sure any new elements you add have a visual alignment with the other items in the page. To provide more white space at the top of the envelope and draw attention to the positioning statement, the logo was dragged closer to the company name. All three elements, were selected and aligned to the left edge using the Element > Align Objects command. The sharp edge that results provides an anchor for the vertical text.

Save the envelope. When you're done customizing your envelope, save your changes. You can use Tripak templates 2000746 and 2000747 to create a business card and letterhead that match this envelope.

Variations: Add horizontal text

If your positioning statement (or any other text you want to add) is an entire sentence or more, it makes sense to add it to the envelope as a horizontal element. The long line of text can be accommodated in the design by adjusting the other elements. You may need to experiment with different alignments to get the look you want.

Add the horizontal text. This positioning statement was added along the bottom of the envelope template. In keeping with the informal tone of the slogan, a casual font was selected and the text was placed in quotes.

Adjust the alignment. To balance the long line of text at the bottom of the envelope visually, the logo and name were moved closer together and dragged to the top of the envelope. The name and address text were aligned flush left using the Type > Alignment command. Finally, all four frames (logo, name, address, and positioning statement) were selected and aligned with the left edge using the Element > Align Objects (Windows) or Element > Align (Mac OS) command.

Alignment is a concept that works equally well for focusing attention and conveying an image. In simple words, it means making sure that everything on a page has a visual connection with something else. You can align the beginning or end of text, the right edges, left edges, or centers of objects, or blocks of text and images. Aligned pages present a stronger image even when the alignment is an invisible line that provides a hard vertical edge.

When elements are separated into blocks to suggest relationships, aligning edges presents a unified appearance.

Stick to one alignment for all the text on a page.

Tools:

Adobe PageMaker Plus

Templates:

*Tripak 2000749,
2000750, 2000751*

Fonts:

*Serpentine and
Bell Gothic*

Project 4

Using Template Sets to Create Stationery

*Rearrange frames in a template set to produce matching cards,
letterhead, and envelopes*

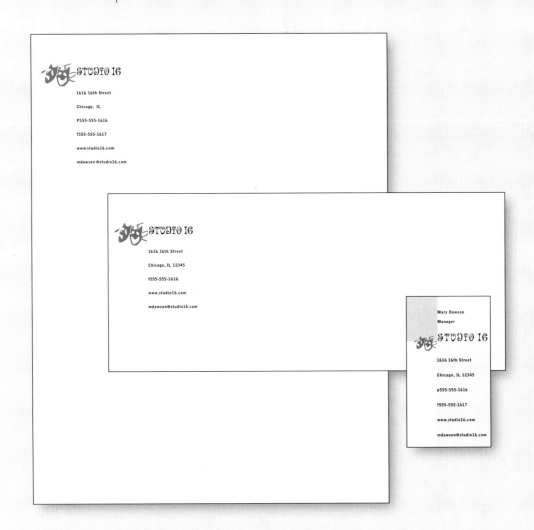

TriPak templates are matched sets of three templates—one for a business card, one for letterhead, and one for an envelope. (Related templates are numbered consecutively in the TriPak folder.) By customizing one template, grouping the elements, and then dragging the group to the other two templates, you can create a professional-looking stationery package in a matter of minutes.

① Getting started. Open TriPak template 2000749 (the business card). Save the template with a new name and turn off the Tips layer.

Just under the name and title, this template has a text frame on the left, a logo in the middle, and another text frame on the right. In this example, the template frames will be rearranged.

Set guides. Before you delete any elements from a template, it's always a good idea to mark their position with guides. Drag a horizontal guide down until it rests along the top of the text and logo placeholders.

Replace the text placeholder with a logo. In this example, we placed the logo to the left of the company name. First we used the pointer (➤) to select the left text frame and deleted it. Then we added our logo and dragged it into position to the left of the existing logo placeholder. Try adding your logo somewhere in the template other than in the original logo placeholder position. For information on adding art, see page 8.

Drag your logo into position using the guides to help you position it. If you need more room for your logo, you can drag the left edge of the logo to the page boundary. This will give you the space you need while maintaining the clean alignment of the template elements.

Type the company name. Since our logo is now on the left, we deleted the logo placeholder, then dragged the remaining text frame to the left until it abutted the logo. Arrange the frames to fit your needs.

Select the text tool (**T**) and type your company name. You may need to increase the width or height of the text frame to fit your name, or you can reduce the font size in the Control palette. To preserve the template alignment, try to keep the company name within the width of the under-lying gray box.

Note: Make sure you use the Control palette to change the text characteristics, instead of modifying the style. If you modify the style, the text will revert to its original settings when you paste it into the other templates later in steps 9 and 10.

Replace the other text in the template. Use the text tool (**T**) tool to select and replace the text in the other two text frames. Notice that when you press Return or the text runs over to the next line, the text frame keeps its spacing.

Delete the second card. Select the pointer and drag a box around all the elements in the second card (you may need to zoom out to get above or below the card). This selects everything inside of the box. Press the Backspace (Windows) or Delete (Mac OS) key to delete the second card placeholder.

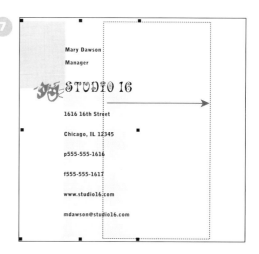

Duplicate and save the card. Drag a box around all the elements in the card you've modified and choose Element > Group so you can duplicate the card as a single unit.

Press Control + Alt (Windows) or Control + Option (Mac OS) to make a copy as you drag the selection to the right. Line up the left edge of the top box with the guide in the middle of the page to position the second card.

Save your business cards leaving the template open. With the card completed, you're ready to copy the elements to the other business pieces.

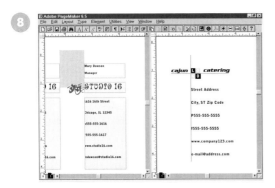

Open the letterhead template. Open TriPak template 2000750 (the letterhead). Save the file with a new name and turn off the Tips layer. Choose Window > Tile to display the business card and letterhead side by side.

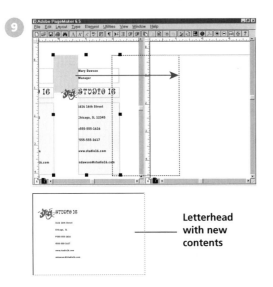

Letterhead with new contents

Copy the contents to the letterhead template. Drag down a horizontal guide until it rests along the top of the text box in the letterhead template.

This template has a vertical and horizontal rule in it. If you want to keep the rules, Shift-click to select all the elements except the rules and delete them. (If you don't want to keep the rules, it's easier to select everything by dragging a box around all the elements and then deleting.)

Return to the business card template. Use the pointer to drag the grouped selection to the letterhead, lining up the top edge of the logo with the horizontal guide. Press the Control key (Windows) or Command (Mac OS) and select the top gray box and the name text frame at the top of the card. (Pressing the Control key or Command key selects just these items and leaves the rest grouped). Delete the box and name frame, then readjust the grouped selection if necessary. Save the letterhead.

Copy the contents to the envelope template. Open TriPak template 2000751 (the envelope). Follow steps 8 and 9 to delete its contents and copy the information from the card to the envelope template. Save the template, and as easy as that, you have a beautiful matched set of stationery!

The repetition of key elements is a powerful way to unify and reinforce your business identity. The primary example of this is your logo—that's why it's important to include your logo on all your business communications. But you can also incorporate consistent elements as part of the design of multiple business pieces (as you did in this project), as part of a multiple page document (such as your newsletter), or within a specific piece. The use of the same typefaces, colors, space relationships, graphics, or slogans can help your customers recognize immediately that a particular piece is from your company, even before they begin reading!

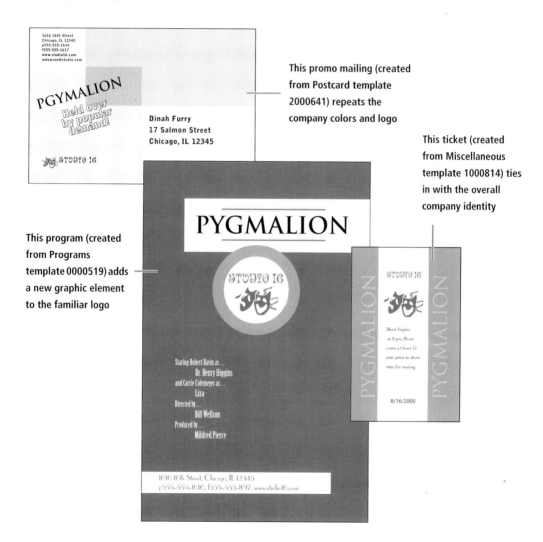

This promo mailing (created from Postcard template 2000641) repeats the company colors and logo

This ticket (created from Miscellaneous template 1000814) ties in with the overall company identity

This program (created from Programs template 0000519) adds a new graphic element to the familiar logo

Tools:

Adobe PageMaker Plus

Templates:

*Business Sets 1000646,
1000649, 1000651*

Fonts:

Goudy

Project 5

Customizing Libraries for Business Sets

Use libraries for easy access to frequently used business elements.

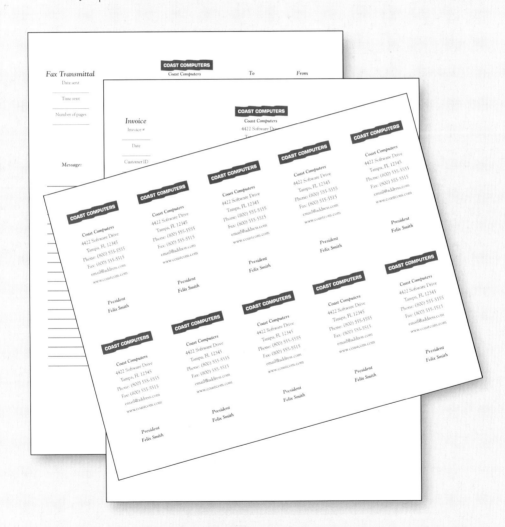

Business Sets templates allow you to customize business forms, such as invoices, statements, purchase orders, and price lists, as well as cards, letterhead, and envelopes. (Related templates are numbered consecutively in the Business Set folder.)

Since you use many of the same elements in all these forms—your logo, company name, phone and fax numbers, mail address, and e-mail address—you can save time by storing these elements in a PageMaker Plus library. Then, when you need one of these items, you simply open the library and drag it into the publication.

Getting started. Open Business Sets template 1000646 (the business card). Save the template with a new name and turn off the Tips layer. (If you already have a business card, go directly to step 3.)

Coast Computers
4422 Software Drive
Tampa, FL 12345
Phone: (800) 555-5555
Fax: (800) 555-5515
email@address.com
www.coastcom.com

President
Felix Smith

Customize the business card template. Use the pointer (➤) to select and delete the placeholder logo and replace it with your logo. Type in your company name, address information, and title.

If you change any text characteristics, use the Control palette (see the Note on page 38). If you need help customizing the business card, see Project 2.

Save your business card.

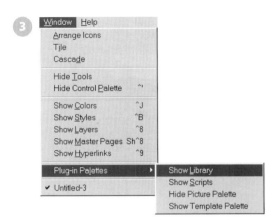

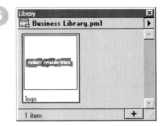

Create a library. Choose Window > Plug-in Palettes > Show Library. Click the triangle on the upper right corner of the palette to display the palette menu and choose New Library. Give your library a name and click Save.

Add an element to your library. Use the pointer to select the element you want to include in the library. For example, we selected the logo in this business card. With the element selected, click the plus sign (+) at the bottom of the Library palette. The element appears in the library.

Name the item. Double-click the library entry and give it a name. You can add other information such as the date, your name, and any keywords or descriptors you might want to use to search for this element.

Add other elements. Select another element and click the plus sign (+) to add it to the library. Do the same for all the elements you want to store in this library. In this example, we placed the company name, address, and title in the Business library. When all the elements are stored in the library, save your library again and close your business card.

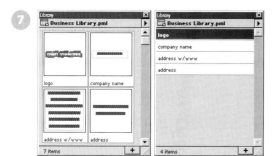

Explore the library views. Currently you're looking at the library in the images and names display. Choose Display images and Display names from the Library palette menu to see other ways of looking at a library.

Use the library elements in other documents. Open Business Sets template 1000649 (the invoice). Use the available guides or create your own to mark the location of the logo and address items on the invoice. Delete the placeholders.

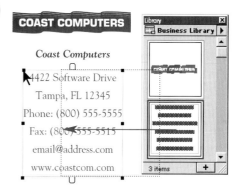

Place the elements in new publications. Select the pointer and drag the logo from the library to the invoice and adjust its postion.(If you need to move the logo just a little bit, you can use the arrow keys on your keyboard to "nudge" it into place.) Now, do the same with the text element. Save and close the invoice.

Open Business Sets template 1000651 (the fax transmittal). Delete the placeholders and drag elements from the library to customize the fax cover sheet. Save the cover sheet.

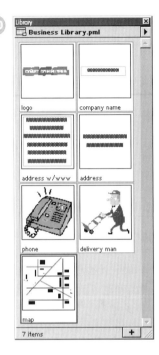

Variation: Build libraries around specific topics

Add to your Business library. If you use other graphics in your brochures, advertisements, or direct mail pieces, you can save a lot of time by storing them in your Business library too. For example, you may have a map that you include instead of written directions. Or, perhaps you include a telephone graphic to emphasize your phone number or a delivery person to indicate fast service.

With these few simple steps, you have the beginning of an entire set of customized business forms!

If you find that you use particular images or clip art from the PageMaker CD frequently, you can store them in libraries too. Then, when you need the art, you won't need to search through the Picture palette or various categories. All the art will be right at hand in a single library.

Nothing works as effectively as a logo to build recognition and confidence in your customers. When you're first starting out, you may not be able to afford a graphic artist to design your logo. The good news is that you can create a simple logo in PageMaker Plus to use in your publications.

Your logo can be anything from your initials to an abstract symbol. The trick is to create a logo that's an immediate and distinctive visual identifier of your company, product, or service.

Logos can be as simple as your initials or company name. For a more graphic effect, try incorporating clip art.

Logos need to be versatile. As part of the design process, print the logo in several sizes. Make sure the logo looks as good in black and white as it does in color.

Tools:
Adobe PageMaker Plus

Templates:
Brochures 1000324

Fonts:
AGaramond

Project 6

Adding Style to Brochures

Use style sheets to format multiple-page documents.

Help Us
Help Them!

Wildlife
Rescue

Everyday, more...

...on...

Migrating Egrets

The problem of suitable stopping and feeding areas for migratory birds is truly a world-wide problem that gets worse with each passing year. As coastal landfill, water diversion, and rampant construction cut down on the traditional migratory rest stops, some private groups have stepped in to save these birds from extinction. Water diversion has lowered the water table so much that previously isolated islands, safe for egg hatching, are now reachable by predators.

Chimpanzees

Once prized for their experimental value and nearly driven to extinction, native populations of chimpanzees are once again reaching a margin of safety. Because of their intelligence and close relationship to homo sapiens, chimpanzees were often the victims of capture for display and research purposes. Wildlife Rescue funds 5 reserve management facilities specializing in recovering and rehabilitating chimpanzees until they can once again return to their natural breeding grounds.

Affliated Organizations
Wildlife Rescue has joined together with the Sierra Club, Preserve Our Heritage Alaskan Foundation, and Forests Forever to strengthen our rescue efforts.

Cheetahs

Wildlife Rescue
31755 Eagle Road
Feather, IA 12345

Bill Ferry
President

Coffee for the birds?
Did you know that the Peruvian Crane may loose it's natural habitat if coffee growers loose their land? That's right. The Peruvian Crane nesting grounds are in the coffee fields in Peru.

Peruvian Crane

Wildlife Rescue

Visit our welsite at www.wildliferescue.com

Style sheets provide a convenient way to make sure your business documents present a consistent image. Especially in multiple page publications, a style sheet can be a real time-saver. For example, using a style for headlines, subheads, and body text means that you don't need to worry about formatting as you enter text. You simply apply the styles when you're ready to finalize the layout.

Another advantage of style sheets is that they let you quickly reformat large amounts of text. Edit a style, and your publication can have a whole new look in seconds.

Getting started. Open Brochures template 1000324. Save the template with a new name and turn off the Tips layer.

This is a two-page template, one for each side of a three-fold brochure. (Template page numbers appear in the lower left corner. The current page is highlighted.)

Delete the placeholders. The right side of page 1 is the cover of the brochure. Scroll to the right, then use the pointer (↖) to select and delete the items you don't need. In this example, all the text placeholders except the brochure name and the company name were deleted, leaving the colored areas. The logo placeholder was also deleted.

Customize the cover. This brochure template has a placeholder for a large piece of art on the cover. Place the art you want to use. (For more information, see "Placing art in a frame" on page 11.) We used the Leopard image (004786.jpg) from the Animals and Insects category.

Replace the title and company name text. Replace the text in the title area, keeping the same style. (If you're unfamiliar with using the Styles palette, see "Changing text styles" on page 13.)

In this example, the title remains in the Heading 1 style. The text in the company name placeholder in its current style (Company Name — Centered) is too small for this cover. We applied the Heading 1 style for the company name as well.

Don't be alarmed if the text seems to disappear when you change a style. Sometimes, when the new font is larger, the text is temporarily hidden. To redisplay hidden text, use the pointer to select the text frame and then drag down the red windowshade at the bottom of the frame.

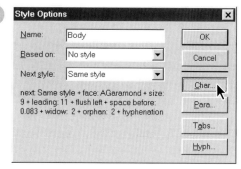

Enter body text. Click the 2 in the lower left corner to move to the inside page of the brochure. Using the text tool (**T**), click in one of the columns of text. You can see that this text is in the Body style. Enter your text in the columns.

Our brochure required less text in each column. As a result, empty space was left at the bottom of each column. Editing the Body style will allow the smaller amount of text to fill the individual text frames.

Change the body style. To edit a style, double-click the style in the Styles palette to display the Style Options dialog box (see page 13).

We wanted to change the text characteristics in the style, so we clicked the Char button. In the Character Specifications dialog box, we increased the font size from 9 to 10 (in general, you don't want body text to be larger than 11 point). We changed the leading from 11 to 13 (leading is the space between the horizontal lines of text in a paragraph).

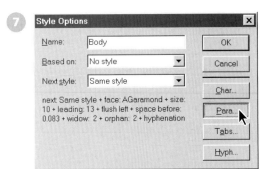

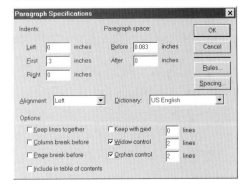

8 **Save your brochure.** Try experimenting with modified character and paragraph characteristics (such as color) for the other styles. When you're done modifying styles, save your brochure.

Indent the first line of each paragraph. We also wanted to indent the first line of each paragraph in the text frames. To make a change that affects the paragraphs in a style, double-click the style and click the Para button in the Style Options dialog box. We changed First indentation to .3 inches. When you click OK, the modified style is automatically applied to the first line in all the paragraphs styled with the Body style.

Variation: Creating a new style

In addition to editing a style, you can also add your own styles to a style sheet. For example, you may want to apply color to specific sections of body text to make them stand out.

1 **Create a new style.** Select the style that's closest to the one you want to create in the Styles palette (in this case the Body style), and then choose New Style from the Styles palette menu.

2

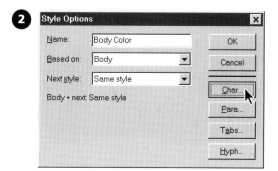

Set the Style options. Name the style Body Color and click the Char button.

3

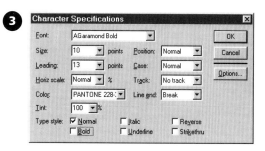

Set the Character options. Choose a new color from the Color menu in the dialog box. To help keep the template consistent, the color menu lists only the colors that are already in the template. In this example, the font was also changed to AGarramondBold.

4

Apply the new style. When you return to the publication, the new style appears in the Styles palette. Select the text you want to change and click the style you created.

Variation: Threading text

This brochure template is designed so that each text frame contains a separate story. When you create your brochure, your stories may require more than one column. To flow the text into an adjoining frame, you use a technique called threading.

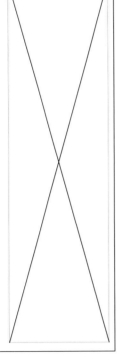

Delete any unthreaded frames. If necessary, draw guides to mark locations, and then select and delete any adjoining unthreaded frames. (You need to make room for the threaded frame.) Select the frame tool (⊠) and draw a new, empty frame next to the original frame.

2 **Edit the text in the frame.** Click the text tool and enter your text in the first frame. As you get to the bottom of the frame and continue typing, the text disappears. It has gone outside the boundary of the frame.

3

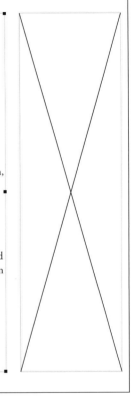

Select the text frame. With the pointer selected, select the text frame you just typed into. You'll see a windowshade at the top and bottom of the frame. The bottom windowshade is red, indicating that there is more text in the frame.

④

Alaskan Bears

From time before time, and the Alaskan natives say, the Alaskan bears lived a peaceful live, free to roam the tundra in the warmer months and hibernate through the frigid Alaskan winters. But encroaching population, random foresting, and the discovery of oil has forever changed the native environment of the bear population. Forced to forge for food farther and farther from its preferred isolated homelands, bears have received the unfair reputation of a man-hunting, vicious scavengers. Wildlife Rescue, in conjunction with the Preserve Our Heritage Alaskan Foundation, has worked to influence state and federal lawmakers to return some of the bear's natural hunting grounds. In addition, education programs, detailing the habits and health needs of these giants of the north, have been instituted in schools and tourist centers. We are happy to report that sightings of bears around inhabited villages and campgrounds has been dropping the last two years as the bears retreat to their preferred terrain.

Thread the text Click the bottom windowshade and the cursor turns into the thread icon (⮞⬚). Click the adjoining frame and the text flows into the new frame.

Tools:

Adobe PageMaker Plus

Templates:

Posters 2000456

Fonts:

AvantGarde, Gothic 13, ITC Kabel Book, Poplar, Tempo Heavy Condensed

Project 7

Producing Powerful Posters

Modify text styles to reflect your business identity.

Sometimes, your design will require that you change the font characteristics in a template. The fonts may be too formal (or casual) for your message, or the amount of text you're using may require a different font for readability. There are several ways to change font settings in PageMaker Plus. This project shows you a few of them.

1 **Getting started.** Open Posters template 2000456. Save the template with a new name and turn off the Tips layer.

This template requires fonts that are not automatically installed with PageMaker Plus. If you see the Font Matching Results dialog box when you open this template, see "Installing fonts for templates" on page 4.

2

Select overlapping frames. The top of this template contains several overlapping frames. To select overlapping frames, use the pointer (➤) and click once (this selects the topmost frame), then hold down the Control button (Windows) or the Command

key (Mac OS) and click again. The next frame down is selected. In this template, you want to select the frame containing the world art, which is used as a logo placeholder.

Here are a few tips to help make selecting overlapping frames a little easier:

• Zoom in on the area that contains the overlapping frames. This lets you see the frame boundaries more clearly.

• Delete all unnecessary frames. If you won't be using a frame, delete it before you start customizing the template.

• Choose View > Hide Guides. This temporarily turns off the ruler guides so you can see the frame boundaries. To turn the guides back on, choose View > Show Guides.

• Watch for the windowshades when selecting text frames. There may seem to be a lot of handles, but only the selected text frame displays a window-shade.

Replace the art. Use the pointer to select and delete the logo placeholder, then add your logo. Select and delete the clip art and replace it with your own art. (For more information, see "Adding art to templates" on page 8.) Save your publication.

In this example, the world graphic was replaced with a round logo and the clip art was replaced with clip art from the Education and People categories. (For more information, see "Locating images and clip art" on page 6.)

Replace the text and change its color. Use the text tool (**T**) to select, delete, and replace the Extra, Yard, and Sale text.

If you have trouble selecting the text, see the tips in Step 2. To select the Extra text, make sure the insertion point is near the top of the word, well away from the Yard text.

Edit the text in the address and subhead areas. To change text color, select the text and click a color in the Colors palette. You'll probably get some unexpected and interesting color changes because of overlapping frames.

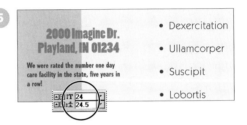

Change text size in the Control palette. If your text doesn't fit, change its size (see the design tip at the end of this project if you need to scale your text to fit). We wanted the address text to be smaller.

When you're modifying a single occurrence of a style or a single text attribute, it's convenient to make the change in the Control palette. To change size, select the text and choose a size from the menu. (To undo a change, just choose the original size from the menu.) You can also change fonts, kerning, tracking, and leading in the Control palette.

6

- Celebrating our 10th year of service!

- Montessori-trained staff

- Ages 3 months to 5 years

- Half and full day sessions

- Individual, personalized attention for every child

- Spacious professionally designed play areas

- Weekly field trips

- Nutritious snacks

- Diverse population

- Scholarships available

Delete a column. This template lists items in two columns. We wanted to use a single column, so we used the pointer to select the right column and deleted it. The remaining column was resized to fill the available space and new text was added.

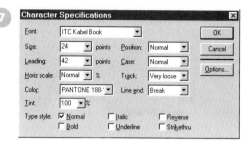

7

Change text size in the Styles palette. Since we added less text than the template called for, the column text needed to be bigger to fill the space. When a style is applied to a lot of text, it's easier to change its attributes using the Styles palette. (For more information on editing styles, see page 13.) We changed the Tab Character style to 24 points.

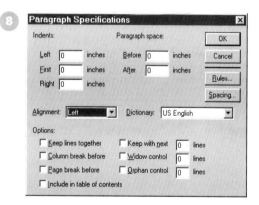

8

Change a paragraph style in the Styles palette. We also wanted to change the alignment of the Address style from right to left. One way to do this is to double-click the style in the Styles palette and change the alignment using the Para button in the Style Options dialog box (see page 13).

There are two other ways to change a paragraph style setting:

• Select the text, choose Type > Paragraph, and modify the settings.

• Select the text and click the paragraph button (¶) in the Control palette, then change the settings.

9 **Change a font using the Character command.** We wanted to experiment with the text in the middle left of the poster (identified as the Subhead style in the Styles palette). Because we wanted to change several attributes, we chose Type > Character.

The Character Specifications dialog box gives you the most control over all aspects of the type and is the best way to change multiple style characteristics at one time. Try changing the font, color, tint, case, and style of the type. When you click OK, all of these attributes are changed at once.

Save and print your poster. You're ready to print and distribute your poster. This poster prints on 8.5 by 17 inch paper.

There will be instances where you want to use the style of a particular headline or subhead, but you have too much or too little text to fit in the frame and still keep the same layout. You can spread out or contract your text using the horizontal scale setting in the Control palette or the Character Specifications dialog box.

Reducing the horizontal scale creates tall, skinny type, so you can fit in more characters. Increasing the scale creates short, fat type. Use horizontal scaling only on large, headline type. Scaling body text makes it too difficult to read.

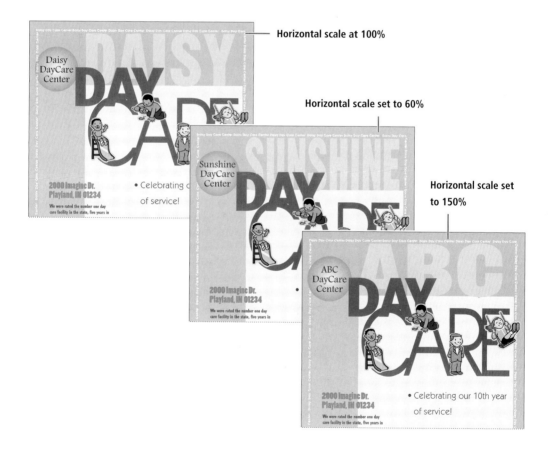

Horizontal scale at 100%

Horizontal scale set to 60%

Horizontal scale set to 150%

Tools:

Adobe PageMaker Plus

Templates:

Ads 2000611

Fonts:

AvantGarde, Myriad Roman, ITC Kabel Ultra, Franklin Gothic

Project 8

Wrapping Text in Advertisements

Grab attention by wrapping text around a graphic.

Wrapping text lends an eye-catching visual impact to an advertisement. Here's an easy way to wrap text around any size or shape graphic.

① **Getting started.** Open Ads template 2000611. Save the template with a new name and turn off the Tips layer.

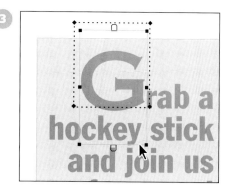

③

②

Adjust the initial cap. If your title text takes up less room (as ours does in this example), you may need to adjust the initial cap. Select the initial cap and drag it to the right to line up the cap with the rest of the text. Use the guides to keep the letters even.

Replace the title text. Use the text tool (**T**) to select the lower case text in the left column and delete it. Enter your own text. Select the initial cap and type in the correct cap for your text.

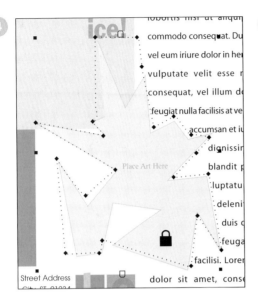

Delete the art placeholder. In this template, the text wraps around an irregular shape. You can adjust the text wrap to fit any piece of art.

Use the pointer to select the art placeholder. The dotted line shows the boundary for the text wrap.

When you select the placeholder, the Apply button (⊗) on the far left of the Control palette loses its button outline, indicating that the selected item is locked. Choose Element >Unlock. Once the element is unlocked, the Apply button (⊠) returns to its usual three-dimensional appearance. Delete the art placeholder.

Add new art. Drag your art into the template and position it near the middle of the page (see page 8). At this point, the art covers up some of the text.

6

Wrap the text. Select the art with the pointer and choose Element > Text Wrap. In the dialog box, choose the center wrap option and set the standoff value. (The standoff determines the distance of the text from each side of the art.) In this example, we used a standoff value of 0. When you click OK, the text wraps around the art.

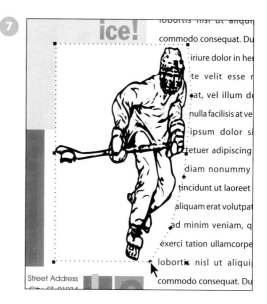

7

Reshape the graphics boundary. To make the text hug your art, click any of the text wrap boundary handles and drag. As you change the shape, the text rearranges to fill the space. To add a new handle, click anywhere on the dotted line. Keep adding handles and dragging them until you have the shape you want.

8 **Replace the body text.** Use the text tool to select and replace the body text.

9

Add your logo and text. Use the pointer to select the logo placeholder, unlock the placeholder using the Element > Unlock command, and delete it. Use the text tool to replace the text in the bottom text frame.

In this example, the text frame was widened so the logo type would fit on one line.

10

Save your advertisement. Click the Save button (⊟) in the toolbar (Windows) or choose File > Save (Mac OS). Your advertisement is now ready to be printed as a flyer, or in a newspaper or newsletter.

Contrast is one of the easiest and most effective ways to add interest to a printed page. You can create contrast in many ways—by the juxtaposition of sizes or shapes, by the sharp variation between dark and light areas, or by a combination of different fonts. In an advertisement, you have only a few seconds to grab the reader's attention. The creative use of contrast is one way to help get your marketing message across.

M agic Cream is a new, exciting breakthrough in the extraction of essential elements from the papaya fruit and has resulted in a revolutionary new lotion. Are your knees, elbows and feet dry and flaky? Have you ever tried every cream on the market? Well, your days of pain and embarrassment are over.

Use different (but complimentary) fonts to create contrast. Using a large drop cap in a different font increases the contrast even more.

Magic Cream is a new, exciting breakthrough in the extraction of essential elements from the papaya fruit and has resulted in a revolutionary new lotion. Are your knees, elbows and feet dry and flaky? Have you ever tried every cream on the market? Well, your days of pain and embarrassment are over.

It's true, this lotion works in only 5 days. In fact, you'll start getting relief with the first application. After years of scientific research, our labs in Pittsland, NJ have proven that this is the most effective reliable way to rejuvenate your skin.

Rub Away Unsightly Wrinkles!

MONEY BACK GUARANTEE!

RUB AWAY

MAGIC CREAM

Frustrated by Itchy, Scaly Skin?
Are your knees, elbows and feet dry and flaky? Have you tried every cream on the market? Well, your days of pain and embarrassment are over. A new, exciting breakthrough in the extraction of

"My skin has never been so smooth and soft." Kate O'Day

Amazing Results in Just 5 Days!
It's true, this lotion works in only 5 days. In fact, you'll start getting relief with the first application. After years of scientific research, our labs in Pittsland, N.J. have proven that

The use of bold reverse type adds contrast to this text-heavy advertisement.

Flowing text around an irregularly shaped graphic contrasts with the square shapes of the text blocks

Tools:
Adobe PageMaker Plus

Templates:
Direct Mail 3000587c

Fonts:
*AGaramond, ITC Fenice,
Zapf Dingbats*

Project 9

Personalizing Direct Mail Letters

Use indents and tabs to set off text.

Whenever your publication contains large blocks of text, as in a letter or report, you can focus attention on key points using tabs and indentation.

1 **Getting started.** Open Direct Mail template 3000587c. Save the template with a new name and turn off the Tips layer.

2

Enter the customer address. Use the text tool (**T**) to enter the customer name and address. In this example, an additional graphic was placed next to the return address. (For information on adding art to a template, see page 8.)

3

Replace the bottom text. To preserve the shadow effect in the bottom text, use the pointer (➤) to select and drag the top text box slightly off the shadow text.

Use the text tool to select the shadow text (the Voucher Headline Shadow style will be highlighted in the Styles palette). Enter the new shadow text.

Select the text in the top text box (the Voucher Headline style will be highlighted) and type the same words. Use the pointer to drag the top text frame back over the shadow text frame and offset it slightly. To alter the amount of shadow, use the arrow keys on your keyboard to move the frame in small increments. We chose to delete all the text below the headline.

Select a paragraph. Zoom in on the paragraph where you want to indent, and select the text using the text tool.

Indent the text. Choose Type > Indents/Tabs. Drag the Indents/Tabs dialog box until the left and right triangles are over the guides along the edges of your text (not the boundary of your document).

Drag the upper and lower left triangles to set the left indentation, then click Apply. Drag the right triangle to set the right indentation and click Apply. (If you can't see the right triangle, click the arrow button at the right edge of the dialog box to move the ruler.)

We set the left indent to 1 inch and the right indent to 5 1/2 inches. The resulting paragraph is indented 1 inch from the left and right margins.

Replace the logo and body text. Use the pointer to select the logo placeholder and delete it. Add your own logo.

Use the text tool to select and delete the body text. Enter all your text in the default Body style, even the text you want to indent or separate with tabs.

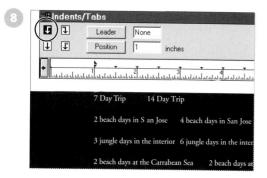

7 Day Trip   14 Day Trip

2 beach days in San Jose   4 beach days in San Jose

3 jungle days in the interior 6 jungle days in the interior

2 beach days at the Carrabean Sea   2 beach days at the Carrabean Sea

Set the tabs in the text. Place the insertion point in the text before the first place where you want to add a tab, and press the Tab key. The text moves to the first default tab marker. (You will set your own tabs in a minute.) In the same line, place the insertion point at the next tab location and press Tab again. Do this for every tab position you want to create.

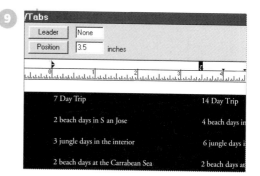

Add the first tab. Select the paragraphs in which you want to insert tabs. Choose Type > Indents/Tabs and drag the dialog box so that the left and right triangles are on the guides along the edges of the text.

Click the left tab alignment icon and then click in the ruler where you want to place the first tab (all the default tabs to the left of this point will disappear).

Click Apply. This example places the first tab at the 1-inch marker. To delete a tab you've placed, drag it off the ruler.

Add the remaining tabs. Click the left tab alignment icon and click the next tab location in the ruler. Click Apply. The second tab in this example is at the 3-inch marker. Set the rest of your tabs.

COSTA RICA FOR $10 A DAY!

This is the trip you've been waiting for. With your sense of adventure and desire of off-the-beaten-path travel experiences, we know you will love this relaxing 14-day journey.

If you mail in your voucher below by August 1, 1999, you will recieve an additional $2 a day off.

COSTA RICA FOR $8 A DAY!

Call today and we'll send you our new brochure outlining the wonders of beautiful beaches, unspoiled forests, and hidden gems of wonder Costa Rica. These trips are filling up fast, so be sure and call today.

7 Day Trip   14 Day Trip

2 beach days in San Jose   4 beach days in San Jose

3 jungle days in the interior   6 jungle days in the interior

2 beach days at the Carrabean Sea   2 beach days at the Carrabean Sea

Save your letter. Save the letter. If you want to create a matching direct mail brochure, select and customize Direct Mail template 3000587a. If you want a matching envelope for your letter, select and customize Direct Mail template 300058b.

Most of the PageMaker Plus templates use two, three, or four Pantone colors. The Pantone color system is widely used by professional designers. If your logo was designed by a graphic artist, it probably uses Pantone colors. For more information on the Pantone color-matching system, see the *Adobe PageMaker 6.5 Plus User Guide*.

You can change the color of text and graphics in the PageMaker templates (or colors in imported TIFF and EPS files) so that they match your logo colors. The Direct Mail templates in this project contain two accent colors, green (Pantone 258-3) and purple (Pantone 171-1). We are going to replace the purple color behind the voucher text with an orange color.

You use the Colors palette to replace colors in a template. If the Colors palette is not showing, choose Window > Show Colors to display the Colors palette. Using this palette, you can change the fill color (the color used for text or inside a frame or object), the stroke color (the border of a frame or of objects you draw in PageMaker), or both the fill and the stroke colors. You can also select a different tint to change the color opacity.

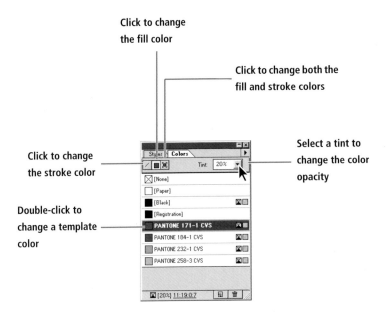

Click to change the fill color

Click to change both the fill and stroke colors

Click to change the stroke color

Double-click to change a template color

Select a tint to change the color opacity

To replace one color with another, first select the object or text you want to change. The current color of the element is highlighted in the Colors palette.

Double-click the color to display the Color Options dialog box. Choose a Pantone library from the Library menu. In the Color Picker, click the color or type in its name. Click OK to close both dialog boxes. The new color appears in the Colors palette, and the color is replaced in the template.

To add a new color rather than replace an existing color, choose New color from the Colors palette menu. Then choose the library in the Color Options dialog box and select the new color in the Color Picker. When you click OK, the new color is added to the Colors palette.

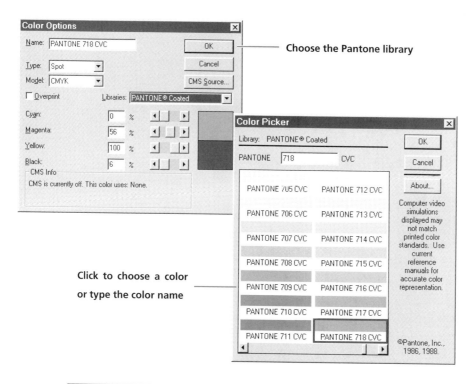

Choose the Pantone library

Click to choose a color
or type the color name

All areas of the template containing the old color are replaced with the new color

Tools:

Adobe PageMaker Plus

Template:

Direct Mail 1000580

Fonts:

Myriad, Giovanni

Project 10

Attracting Attention with Self-Seal Mailers

Spice up your publications with unusual shapes.

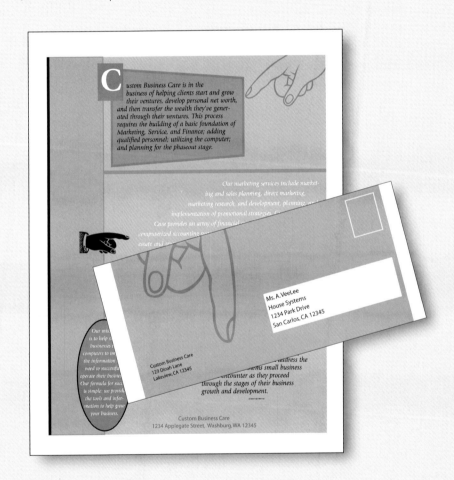

In most publications, text and art appear in rectangular or square blocks. But when you want to catch your readers' attention and compel them to act, try putting text in unusually shaped frames. Text in distinctive shapes particularly complements big, bold graphics.

Getting started. Open Direct Mail template 1000580. Save the template with a new name and turn off the Tips layer.

This is a two-page template. The first page contains the address and the outside fold. The second page contains the mailer text.

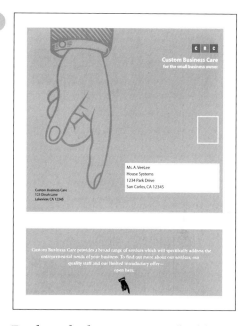

Replace the logo, name, and address placholders. Use the pointer (↖) to select and delete the logo and replace it with your logo (see page 8). Use the text tool (**T**) to select and replace the text in the company name and address frames. (If you're using labels, you can delete the return address and addressee frames.)

3

Call Today. Sale ends June 15, 1999.
First come, first served!

Match the text to its shape. The bottom of the first page uses a unique text frame designed to look like the flap of an envelope. Since the back of a mailing is where most people look first, this is a perfect place to deliver your most important message.

If your message is short, increase the font size so that the text still fills the shape. In this example, the text size was increased to 24 and the leading was set to 26. For information on editing text characteristics, see "Changing text styles" on page 13. We also centered the text.

4

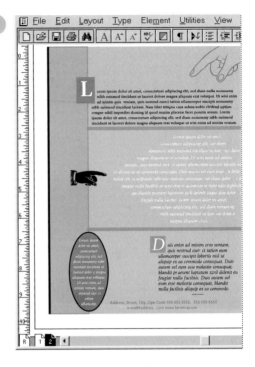

Move to page 2. Click the 2 at the bottom left of the page to move to the inside page. Notice the unique shapes of the text frames in the middle and bottom sections.

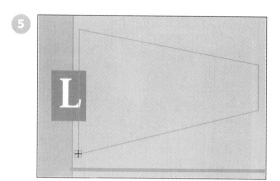

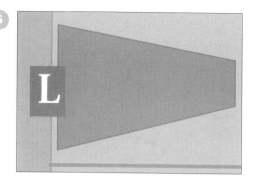

Create a polygon frame. You can easily modify the shape of these frames to fit your company identity and individual text needs. To replace the rectangular shape at the top of the page, we selected and deleted the rectangular frame. Using the polygon frame tool (⊗), we drew a new frame. When you draw a polygon, you click to set the initial point, then add additional points to define the shape. To complete a polygon, click on the first point again.

When you've drawn the polygon, use the pointer to select it and then choose Element > Send to Back to move the polygon behind the drop cap.

Stroke and fill the frame. To add a border around the polygon, choose Element > Stroke and choose a line thickness. To add color to the stroke, click the stroke box (✐) in the Color palette and click a color. To change the fill, click the fill box (□) in the Color palette, then click a color. For more information on using the Color palette, see "Changing template colors" on page 14.

Enter text. Use the text tool to enter your text in the new frame.

8

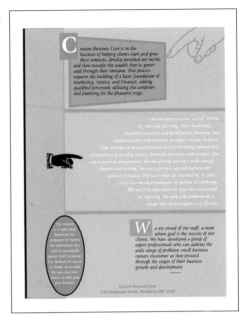

Adjust the shape of the polygon. To adjust the polygon to fit your text, select the pointer and double-click the frame. Small boxes appear at the points you set when drawing the polygon. Drag a point to change its position or click the frame edge to add a new point. Experiment until the frame is the shape you want.

9

Save your self-seal mailer. After you've edited the shapes and entered your own text, you're ready to print the self-seal mailer. This template is designed to print on Avery SKU #8325. To find out more about printing on Avery stock, see the input/output tip at the end of Project 2.

Variation: Using the frame tools

In addition to the polygon frame tool, the PageMaker Plus toolbox also includes tools for drawing rectangular and elliptical frames. (The frame tools have an X in them.) You can use any of these shapes to contain text and frame art.

Draw an elliptical frame. Double-click the ellipse frame tool (⊗). In the dialog box, you can set the fill and stroke colors before you begin drawing. Choose the frame settings and click OK, then draw the ellipse.

To change the settings after you've drawn the ellipse, choose Element > Fill, Element > Stroke, or Element > Fill and Stroke. To change the color of the frame quickly, click the stroke or fill box in the Colors palette, then click a different color.

Variation: Using the drawing tools

When you want to add decorative objects to your publication (as opposed to framing text or art), you use the drawing tools. You can draw lines, rectangles, ellipses, and polygons. (For more on drawing with the polygon tool, see Project 1.)

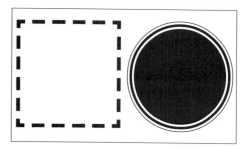

Draw squares and circles. To draw a square or circle, hold down Shift as you drag with the rectangle drawing tool (□) or the ellipse drawing tool (○). (Holding down Shift works when you want to draw square and circular frames too.)

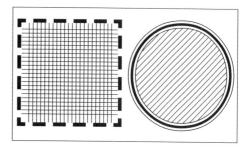

Fill a shape with a pattern. To fill a shape with a pattern, draw the shape and choose Elements > Fill. Choose a pattern from the menu.

Tools:

Adobe Page Maker Plus

Templates:

Reports 30000594

Fonts:

AvantGarde

Project 11

Using Master Pages to Format Reports

Create a consistent layout for multipage publications using master pages.

Master pages provide a cohesive look for multiple-page documents. Placing common elements such as logos, chapter titles, headers, footers, and page numbers on a master page ensures that your pages stay consistent throughout the document. Master pages can also contain nonprinting design elements like column guides, ruler guides, and margin guides.

You can have several master pages in a single publication. For example, a long report might have multiple master pages for different sections. If you want to make changes to your layout, you simply edit the master page; all the pages using this master page are changed automatically.

① Getting started. Open Reports template 3000594. Save the template with a new name and turn off the Tips layer.

This is a three-page template. The first page is the report cover, the second is a table of contents, and the third is the body of the report.

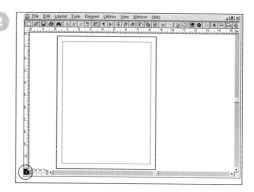

View the master page. Choose Window > Show Master Pages. This palette lists all the master pages in the publication. By default, every publication has a document master. Single pages have a right master page. Click the R (for right) in the lower left corner of the publication window to see the current master page. This master page contains only the margins and orientation for the page.

Modify the layout for the new master page. We're going to make a master page for the body pages of this report. Click the 3 at the bottom left of the publication to move to the body page. This will be the model for the new master page.

Type in your company name and add your logo to the two bottom frames. Because we knew we wanted longer columns for our text, we deleted the art placeholder and did not use a logo. We then used the pointer (➤) to select the rule running down the middle of the page. Shift-dragging the rule allowed us to keep the rule straight as we extended it to the bottom of the columns.

Select the elements you want on the master page. Select the pointer and Shift-click to select the company name, logo, column guides, rule, colored boxes, and any other items you want on every body page.

We did not choose to include the title boxes, the horizontal rule, or the green boxes along the side of the page because we did not want them to appear on every page. If you want to include these frames running along the right edge of the page, Shift-Control-click (Windows) or Shift-Command-click (Mac OS) twice to select both the text frame and the underlying colored frame.

⑤ Choose Edit > Copy. Copy the selected elements to the Clipboard.

⑥

Create a new master page. Choose New Master Page from the Master Pages palette. Name the page and click OK (Windows) or Create (Mac OS). A blank master page appears, and the new master page appears in the Master Pages palette.

⑦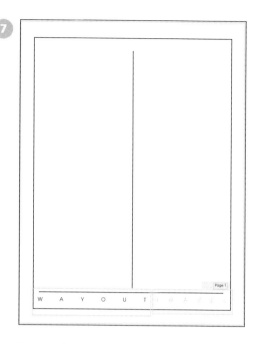

Paste the items into the new master page. Choose Edit > Paste to paste the selected items on the master page. Adjust their position if necessary.

8

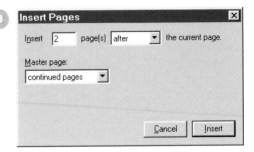

Add page numbering. To number the pages automatically, zoom in on the bottom right of the master page. Select the text tool (**T**) and place the insertion point in the bottom colored square (which currently says Page 1). Select and delete the Page 1 text. Press Control+Alt+P (Windows) or Command+Option P (Mac OS) to replace the number with RM. Page numbers appear as RM (right master) or LM (left master) on the master pages but display the number on the individual pages.

9

Add more pages. To create additional body pages, return to page 3 of the publication. Choose Layout > Insert Pages. Enter the number of pages and make sure the new master page is chosen. Click Insert.

You can also add pages using the Document > Setup command. When you add pages with this command, new pages are added at the end of the publication, and the document master is applied to them.

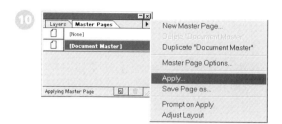

Applying master pages. To apply a master page to a single page, move to the page, then click the master page in the Master Pages palette.

To apply a master page to several pages at one time, choose Apply from the Master Pages palette. In the dialog box, select the Master page and enter the page range.

When you apply a master page, it may be necessary to change the page layout slightly to accommodate the new master page elements. If you want the objects and guides on the page to be repositioned or resized as needed by the new master, click Adjust Layout in the Apply Master dialog box. For more information on the Adjust Layout option, see the *Adobe PageMaker 6.5 Plus User Guide*.

Save your report. Enter the text and art in your report, using any of the master pages. When you save the report publication, your master pages are automatically saved also.

Variation: Creating a master page from an existing page.

The third page in this template, which we modified for the body pages, is designed as a section or chapter opener. You might want to make an additional master page for this publication that contains the title and art placeholder on this page.

Return to page 3 in the publication and choose Save Page As from the Master Pages palette menu. Name the new master page and click Save. The new master appears in the Master Pages palette.

Your PageMaker Plus files can easily be saved in Adobe Acrobat Portable Document Format (PDF). Two great uses of PDF files are distributing a report for review and sending your files to a quick-print shop.

Distributing files in PDF

Reports are one of those publications that often need to be reviewed by others. When you send out a review copy as PDF, your reviewers can easily open and read the document no matter what kind of word processor, fonts, or computer system they use.

Create a PDF file

1 Start Acrobat Distiller 4.0 and set the Job Options:

◯ Choose ScreenOptimized if the reviewer will be reading the report on the Web or intranet, or if you're sending the report as an e-mail attachment.

◯ Choose PrintOptimized if the reviewer will be printing out the report.

◯ Choose PressOptimized if the report is intended for high-quality output.

2 Return to PageMaker Plus and click the Acrobat button in the toolbar (Windows) or choose File > Export > Adobe PDF (Mac OS).

3 In the dialog box, make sure Distill Now is selected. Enter the page range. (In Mac OS, select the View PDF using option.)

4 Deselect Override Distiller Options. (To display this option in Windows, first choose Miscellaneous from the menu at the top of the dialog box.)

5 Select Embed All Fonts. (To display this option in Windows, first choose Format and Fonts from the menu at the top of the dialog box.)

6 Click Export.

7 Name the PDF file and click Save.

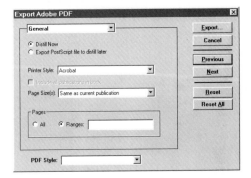

PageMaker Plus automatically opens Distiller and creates the PostScript® file. Acrobat Reader opens so you can proof the PDF file before you send it out.

Don't forget to send along a copy of Acrobat Reader or direct reviewers to the Adobe Web site (www.adobe.com) so they can download their own copy of Acrobat Reader.

Sending PDF files to the printer

More and more printers are using PDF files as their format of choice for electronic submission of print jobs. PDF files can easily be sent as e-mail attachments or uploaded to a Web site for easy retrieval. PDF files remove the necessity of including extra fonts or layout specifics or the need for specific page layout applications because all the formatting is captured within the file itself.

When submitting print jobs electronically, be sure you create the PDF files so that they are optimized for printing (see Step 1 on the previous page). You will also want to set the other general job options, including compression, fonts, and colors. For complete instructions, see the online help for Acrobat Distiller. When preparing your files for electronic submission, be sure to check with your printer before sending the job.

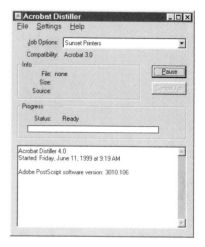

Some service providers have created Distiller profiles that provide all the information you need to create your PDF file. If your printer sends you a profile, place it in the Settings folder in the Distiller folder.

When you open Distiller, select the profile you received from the print shop in the Job Options menu. All the Distiller settings are changed to fit this profile.

Tools:

Adobe PageMaker Plus

Templates:

Newsletters 1000369

Fonts:

AGaramond,
Franklin Gothic

Project 12

Entering Newsletter Text Using the Story Editor

Enter and edit large blocks of text using the story editor.

Downtown Investments

Volume 26, Issue 7, Summer 1999

The Year 2000
How will it effect you?

Christopher Lee

Better planning your financial future starts.

Back in the 1940's, when they were working on the first vacuum-tube computer, the pioneering engineers at IBM didn't think about the year 1999. Who knew, during that war-filled time, if humans, let alone the machine they were designing, would still be around 60 years later. Yet, here we are, with less than 18 months to go before the familiar prefix, 19 disappears forever. In the last few years, there has been many unique approches to solving the unexpected digital problem.

Wall Street, New York, itself one of the prime players in this time drama, has been researching and preparing its brokers for the coming millennium. It is now preparing guidelines for new installation. You can check your brokers web site for more specific information, but suffice it to say that most companies have a good handle on what changes in coding are required.

Six easy steps to increasing your portfolio return. Make your investments grow with little investement of your time. There is no need to spend countless hours of your precious time working on making your money grow.

"Will Wall Street survive the change?"

Back in the 1940's, when they were working on the first vacuum-tube computer, the pioneering engineers at IBM didn't think about the year 1999. Who knew, during that war-filled time, if humans, let alone the machine they were designing, would still be around 60 years later. Yet, here we are, with less than 18 months to go before the familiar prefix, 19 disappears forever.

In the last few years, there has been a big push to find a solution to the digit problem. ■

WE CAN SAVE YOU TIME AND MONEY!

In today's bustling world, no doubt the Deni Construction Company keeps you very busy. We also realize that making the correct financial planning decisions is an important part of assuring security for your family and your business. At Financial Care, Inc./Downtown, we're here to provide you the personal service you deserve. Ms. Jody Ryan, one of our top investment consultants, is a specialist in the needs of small businesses like your own. She will do the research, compare the options, and then sit down with you, AT YOUR PLACE OF BUSINESS, to go over your personal investment and financial plan.

If you prefer to do your own research, or have some particular stocks, mutual funds, or other investment priorities, Ms. Ryan will be happy to provide all the technical support you need to carry out your plan. We are a full-service financial planning firm, and we work with you to help you achieve your individual financial goals. At Financial Care, Inc./Downtown, we're here to provide you the personal service you deserve. Ms. Jody Ryan, one of our top investment consultants, is a specialist in the needs of small businesses like your own. ■

FINANCIAL CARE, INC.

DOWNTOWN

125 Center Street
Pleasant Valley,
Utah 91234
Tel: 123 555 1267
Fax: 123 555 1268
www.fincare.com

Volume 26, Issue 7

PageMaker Plus provides two ways to edit text. When you're working in a template, you're in the layout view. In the layout view, you use the text tool to select and replace text. You see immediately how your edits effect the page layout.

To edit large blocks of text, it's faster to work in the story editor (the built-in word processor). You'll learn how to use the story editor in this project.

This project assumes you're familiar with the Style palette. If you haven't used the Style palette before, see "Changing text styles" on page 13.

Getting started. Open Newsletters template 1000369. Save the template with a new name and turn off the Tips layer.

This is a four-page template, a common size for newletters. Four pages require a lot of text!

Replace the art. The cover of the newsletter has placeholders for art and a logo. Use the pointer (↖) to select and delete the logo and replace it with your logo. Place your own art in the art placeholder. For help with placing art, see page 11.

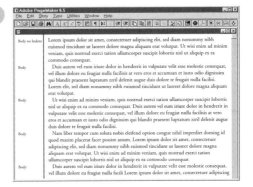

Replace small blocks of text. Select the text tool (**T**) and then select and replace the masthead, headline, byline, caption, and pullquote. For help with replacing text, see page 12.

Place the insertion point in the first paragraph of the text. The Styles palette identifies this as the Body no Indent style. Place the insertion point in the second paragraph. This is the Body style, the style used for most of the newsletter text.

Open the story editor. To switch between the layout view and the story editor, you use the commands in the Edit menu. Choose Edit > Edit Story.

A story is similar to an article in a newspaper. The story editor contains all the text for the currently selected story. In this template, each text frame contains a single story.

Text in the story editor appears with no formatting; this makes it quicker to edit a lot of text. The formatting is still there, however. Place the insertion point in the first paragraph, and you'll see that the Body no Indent style is again highlighted in the Style palette.

You can apply formatting in the story editor by placing the insertion point in a word or paragraph and clicking a style in the Styles palette. You won't see the formatting until you return to the layout view.

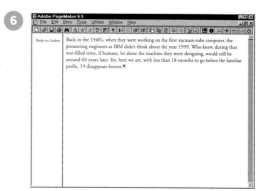

Turn on paragraph marks. When you're working in unformatted text, it's helpful to know where the paragraphs end and where there are blank lines. Choose Story > Display (¶) Marks. The story editor displays the marks at the end of each paragraph and the spaces between words and paragraphs.

Changing body text. Edit the placholder text for this story. You can use all the standard word processing techniques in the story editor. Unless you want to preserve the individual paragraphs or the story length, it's probably easiest to choose Edit > Select All and delete all the placeholder text before you start entering your own text. (Remember to style the first paragraph as Body no Indent and the remaining paragraphs as Body before returning to the layout view.)

⑦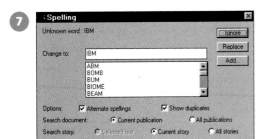

Check the spelling. One of the major advantages of editing in the story editor is that you can check your spelling. Choose Utilities > Spelling to display the Spelling dialog box. If you need help with the spelling options, see the *Adobe PageMaker 6.5 Plus User Guide*.

⑧

Return to the layout view. Choose Story > Edit Layout to return to the template. You'll see your text in the text frame.

Edit the text and add art for the remaining pages. Click the numbers in the lower left corner of the publication to move from page to page. Use the text tool to replace small blocks of text and use the story editor for larger stories. Place your own art in the art placeholders or create your own frames.

Save your newsletter. Click the Save button (📩) in the toolbar (Windows) or choose File > Save (Mac OS). You can print your newsletter on a preprinted masthead or on your stationery. For larger runs, you'll probably want to take the newsletter to a print shop. Check with your printer for art requirements before you bring in your newsletter.

Variation: Placing existing text in a text frame

Especially when you're writing a newsletter, there will be times when you want to reproduce text that already exists in another document. For example, the text may be from a press release, an employee biography, or an e-mail message.

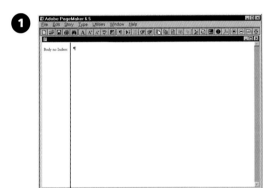

Delete the placeholder text. Place the insertion point in the text frame where you want to place the new text. Choose Edit > Edit Story to open the story editor.

Place your text. Click the Place button (▣) in the toolbar (Windows) or choose File > Place (Mac OS). Navigate to the file you want to import. (In Windows, if you don't see the file you want to open, make sure the Files of Type option in the Place dialog box is set to Importable Files.)

Select the file, click the Replacing Entire Story option, and then click Open. Depending on the type of file you're opening, you may see a dialog box (click OK to accept the default import settings) or an importing message. The new text appears in the story editor.

When your stories are short, you may need to fill up space in your newsletter. The easiest way to do this is to add photos, clip art, additional quotes, or other graphic elements.

Photos are always a good way to break up large blocks of text. You can use the images from the PageMaker Plus CD or photos you've scanned yourself. If you have lots of space, use an unusual frame to set off the photo.

When you want to draw attention to specific text, such as a table of contents, you can enclose the text in a border or put it inside of a shape.

You don't have to fill every inch of a page. Leaving areas of white space makes a page more inviting and emphasizes key points. White space can also serve as an effective organizer of related information.

Adobe PageMaker Plus
Adobe Photoshop 5.0 LE

Templates:

Label Sets 1000775

Fonts:

Goudy

Project 13

Using Layers to Design CD Labels

Use layers to try out different combinations of text and graphics.

PageMaker layers are like transparent sheets of film, one stacked on top of the other. Where there is something on a layer, it blocks out the underlying layers. Where there is nothing on a layer, you can see through to the other layers. You can use layers to try out different combinations of text and graphics, until you get just the right effect.

1 **Getting started.** Open Label Sets template 1000775. Save the template with a new name and turn off the Tips layer.

2

Jubilant Recordings

Replace the logos and text placeholders. Use the pointer (⬉) to select and delete the logo placeholders and replace them with your logo (see page 8). There is a logo placeholder at both the top and the bottom of the template.

Use the text tool (**T**) to select and replace the company name (both top and bottom), the headline, and the text below the headline. Replace the text in the vertical bars on the sides and the text on the back of the label (see page 12).

3

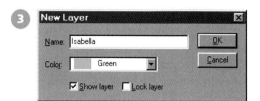

Create a new layer. All the PageMaker Plus templates have two layers, the Tips layer and a Default layer. (If the Layers palette is not showing, choose Window > Show Layers.) The Default layer contains the text and art placeholders. The Default layer is highlighted in the Layers palette, indicating that this is the layer you're working on.

To create a layer, choose New Layer from the Layer's palette menu. In the dialog box, name the layer (in this example, we named it for the Isabella font, which will be applied to the text). Click OK, and the new layer appears at the top of the Layers palette.

④

Copy the logo and text to the new layer. Shift-click with the pointer to select the text frame and the logo, and then choose Edit > Copy. Click the new layer in the Layers palette (so that it's highlighted). Press the Alt key (Windows) or the Option key (Mac OS) and choose Edit > Paste. The copied logo and text appear on top of the originals. Use the text tool (**T**) to select the text and apply a new font (we chose the Isabella font).

⑤

Switch between the two layers. To see the text in the different fonts, hide the Default layer by clicking the eye icon to the left of the Default layer in the Layers palette. To see the original, click the eye icon again to show the Default layer, and then click the eye icon to the left of the new layer to hide it. Showing and hiding layers is how you see your alternative layout designs.

⑥

Put your art on layers. Create another new layer and name it (in our example, Musician Gold). Select the layer so that it is highlighted and place your art on the layer (see page 10). We used the Violinist image (0002726.ai) from the Recreation and Leisure category. Position the image under the company name.

Create another new layer and name it (in this example, Musician Purple). Drag another piece of art to this layer. Our alternative art is the Trumpet Player image (0002729.ai) from the Recreation and Leisure category.

7 **Try out your combinations.** Experiment with the design by showing and
hiding the layers. You can also add
other text (such as song titles or
credits) to one or more of the layers.

This is a simple example of the power of
layers. You can also use layers to try out
different backgrounds, logos, or any
other elements in your publication.

To hide all the layers quickly, click and
drag through the left column of the
Layers palette.To show all the layers,
drag through the column again.

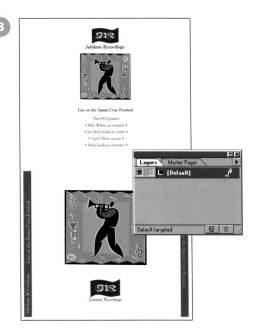

Delete and merge layers. When
you're happy with your layout, delete
the layers you no longer need by
dragging them to the Trash in the
Layers palette. To merge the remaining
layers into the Default layer, select the
Default layer first, then select the layers
you want to use. Press the Control
button (Windows) or the Command
key (Mac OS) and choose Merge
Layers from the Layers palette.

9 **Save and print your labels.** Save
your CD label and print it. This
template is designed to be printed on
Avery SKU #8931. For more information on using Avery products, see
the input/output tip at the end of
Project 2.

There are many sources for royalty-free clip art in stores or on the Web. If you want to use black-and-white clip art, but want it to have the impact of color, you can open the art in Photoshop LE and color it. You can then place the colorized art in your PageMaker publication.

Open your clip art in Photoshop 5.0 LE

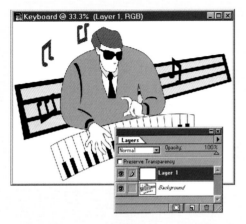

Photoshop LE has the same kind of layers as PageMaker. You can use a layer to test new colors for your clip art. Open the clip art in Photoshop LE and create a new layer by choosing New Layer from the Photoshop LE Layers palette.

Add color to the layer

Pick a color from the Swatches palette to make it your foreground color, then choose Select > All. Choose Edit > Fill and fill the layer with the Foreground color. The new color will completely cover up the art. Choose Select > None.

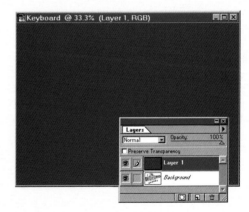

Save the file and place it in PageMaker

Choose File > Save a Copy and choose the EPS format. In PageMaker, choose File > Place and open the file.

Use a blending mode

You can use a Photoshop blending mode to color parts of the art. In the Layers palette, choose Overlay from the Mode menu. Try out different opacities until you get a tint you like. The opacity in this example is set to 80%. You can also experiment with the other blending modes for different effects.

Tools:
Adobe PageMaker Plus

Templates:
Menus 3000500

Fonts:
AvantGarde

Project 14

Adjusting Layout for Menus

Adjust page size, margins, and color to meet your requirements.

When you want to change the output settings for a template, such as increasing the margins or decreasing the paper size, you change the document settings. In this example, a full-color, legal-sized menu is modified to print on letter-size paper using a black-and-white printer.

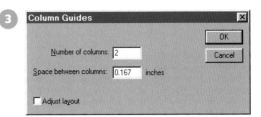

① **Getting started.** Open Menus template 3000500. Save the template with a new name and turn off the Tips layer.

②
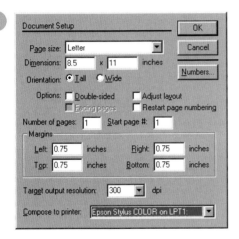

Change the page size and margins. Select File > Document Setup. Choose the new paper size from the Page size menu. Choosing Letter changed the dimensions of this template to 8.5 by 11 inches and also changed the margins. We changed Left Margin to .75 so that it matched the other margins.

Create column guides. Because of the change in margin size, the frames in the page need to be resized.

To help reposition the text in the bottom of the menu, we used column guides. Column guides create columns of equal size that fit between the margins. To add these guides, choose Layout > Column Guides. We changed Number of columns to 2.

④

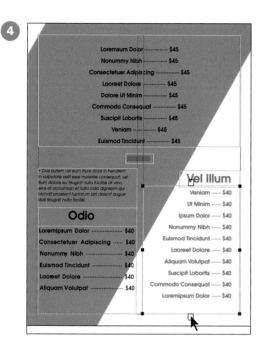

Resize the frames. Use the pointer (↖) to resize the frames so that they fit on the new page size. Starting with the large text frame on the top, we lined up the frame edges using the margin guides. We then aligned the inside and outside edges of the bottom text, using the column guides, and shortened the bottom frames until their lower edges lined up with the bottom guide. Finally, we fit the colored frames inside the new margins.

As you resize the frames, you might want to check periodically how the reformatted document will look when it's printed. Choose View > Hide Guides to remove the guides temporarily. Choose View > Show Guides again to turn the guides back on as you continue to make adjustments.

⑤

Move the title. Next we used the pointer to drag the title text frame down so that the top of the frame lined up with the top guide. We dragged the frame's side handle to make the frame the same width as the text frame below it.

⑥

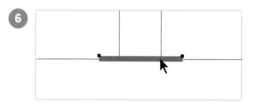

Move the bottom rule. There are two rules in this template, one in the middle of the page and one at the bottom. We selected the bottom rule and dragged it up so it would fit inside the new margins.

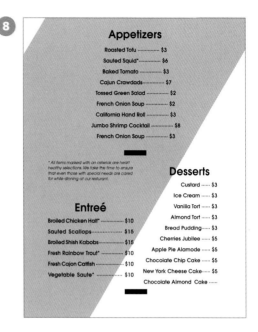

Replace the menu text. Use the text tool (**T**) to select and delete the menu text. Enter your own text.

Change the color elements for black-and-white printing. To prepare the menu for black-and-white printing, we used the pointer to select the orange color swipe. We clicked Black in the Colors palette and adjusted the tint to 30%. (For information on changing template colors, see page 14.)

The green type in the lower right and the two blue bars will probably print fine on the black-and-white printer. If you want to remove all color from the template, however, drag the blue, green, and orange colors to the trash in the Colors palette. Click OK when you're asked if you want to turn the tints to black.

9 **Save the publication.** Click the Save button (▣) in the toolbar (Windows) or choose File > Save (Mac OS). You're ready to print the menu on your black-and-white laser printer.

Variation: Add border text

You can make good use of the empty space around the edges of this menu by adding text. We added the restaurant name.

1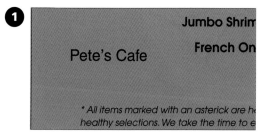

Type the name. Select the text tool (**T**), click near the left edge of the menu, and type the text. Use the Control palette to format the text. Change the font to Avant Garde Bold so that it matches the rest of the text and choose the largest size possible. If you need help with formatting text, see "Changing text styles" on page 13.

2

Rotate the text. To place the text in the border, use the pointer to select the text box and enter 90 in the Rotating option (○) in the Control palette. Drag the handle to increase the text box length so that the text fits on one line and fills the space.

3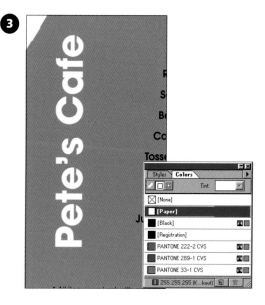

Reverse the type. If you're printing on color stock (see the input/output tip at the end of this project), you can add a nice finishing touch by reversing the border text. Use the text tool to select the text and click Paper in the Colors palette. This setting makes the text the same color as the paper. When you click outside of the text, it appears in reverse type.

One way to save on printing costs and still produce a two-color publication is to print on colored paper. For example, suppose Pete's Cafe is painted blue and has blue checkered tablecloths. The menu is printed on blue paper to reinforce this business identity.

1   If you haven't already done so, delete the blue, orange, and green from the template by dragging the colors to the trash in the Colors palette. All the text and the background swipe will be in black (unless you've already changed the tint for the background).

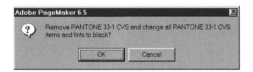

2   Do a test print. Depending on your laser printer, the background may be too dark. If so, use the pointer to select the color swipe and choose a lighter tint from the Tint menu in the Colors palette. We changed the tint to 10%.

3   Load your colored stock and print the menu.

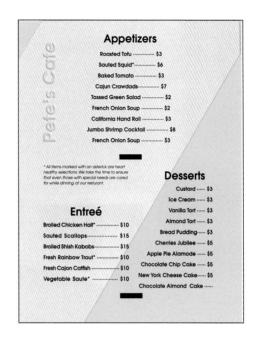

Tools:
Adobe PageMaker Plus

Templates:
Miscellaneous 000815

Fonts:
Myriad,
American Typewriter

Project 15

Creating Image Masks on Tickets

Mask images using drawn shapes.

The same drawing tools you use to create shapes (see Project 10) can also be used to mask images. (A mask covers up part of the underlying object so that only a portion of it shows through the shape.) Masks are another effective way to focus attention on a particular area of a template.

Getting started. Open Miscellaneous template 0000815. Save the template with another name and turn off the Tips layer.

Delete the logo and unnecessary text frames. Zoom in so you can work on one ticket. Use the pointer (**⬆**) to select the logo and delete it. We did not include a logo on the ticket, but you may want to add your logo (for more information on adding art, see page 8). We also deleted the Christmas text frame.

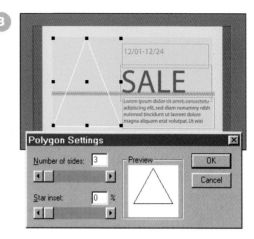

Draw a shape for the mask. In this example, we used a triangle to mask the image. Choose a drawing tool for the mask. Double-click the tool and set the drawing options. We used the polygon tool (○) and set Number of sides to 3. We then stroked the shape with 1 point using the paper color. For more information on using the drawing tools, see Project 10. Don't worry about the exact size of the shape now, you can adjust it after you've placed your image.

Add your image. Follow the instructions on page 8 to bring your art into the template. We used the Arc de Triomphe image (00004607.jpg) from the Images/Travel & Destinations category. The image was resized until it was slightly larger than the triangle.

Move the image backward. To place the image behind the shape, choose Element > Arrange> Send Backward. Use the pointer to resize or move the image until the portion you want to show is enclosed by the shape.

Create the mask. Hold down Shift and use the pointer to select the image *and* the triangle. Choose Element > Mask. The area outside the shape is no longer visible.

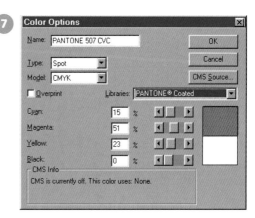

Create a new color. We wanted to change the ticket background color so that it picked up one of the image colors. To add a new color to a template, choose New Color from the Color palette menu. In the Color Options dialog box, chose a library and then select a color. We choose type 507 from the Pantone Coated library. When you click OK, the new color appears in the Colors palette.

8

Change the ticket colors. If you want to change the background color of the ticket, use the pointer to select the lime green frame and the red boxes on each edge of the ticket. Click the stroke/fill box (▣) in the Colors palette and click the new color. We also changed the dark green frame and the horizontal line to black and set the tint to 100%. (For information on changing template colors, see page 14.)

9

Modify the text. Select the top text frame and type in your text. We dragged the text frame up and changed the text color to black with a tint of 50%.

Enter the text in the other frames and adjust the frames as necessary. We enlarged the frame containing the word Sale and changed its font size to 24 in the Control palette. To reverse the type on this dark background, we selected the text and clicked the Reverse style option (▣) in the Control palette. We then moved the horizontal rule up until it separated the two words.

For the text in the lower frame, we chose Type > Alignment > Align Right and changed it to black. We then entered and reversed the text along the bottom of the ticket.

10 **Save, duplicate, and print your tickets.** Click the Save button (▣) on the toolbar (Windows) or choose File > Save (Mac OS). This template is designed to print on Avery stock, SKU #8373, which prints eight duplicate tickets on a page. (See Project 2 for information on duplicating and printing multiple items on a single page.)

Variations: Creating unusual masks

Using the mask option with various shapes and options can give you a wide selection of designs to play with.

Mask with a starburst. The polygon tool allows you to create a lot of different starburst shapes (vary the number of sides and the Star insert value to experiment with different shapes). This starburst has Number of sides set to 23 and Star Inset set to 21. If you want to constrain the starburst, Shift-drag as you draw.

Place the mask behind the object. Create a masking object that contains a fill and choose an object to be masked that contains transparent areas. Choose Elements > Arrange > Send Backward to move the mask behind the object. The fill will show through the transparent areas of the object.

Changing the colors of a template can be one of the most exciting challenges in creating your publication. Sometimes the colors may be dictated by your logo or the theme of the piece. When you have the freedom to pick and choose your colors, it's helpful to think in terms of complimentary colors. Designers use a standard color model that assumes all the primary colors are arranged in a circle. You can use the color wheel as a beginning point for mixing and matching the colors in your templates. Always remember to try out your text on the background color before making final choices. If the text is not easily readable, your message will be lost no matter how compelling the colors are.

Yellow and blue are opposite on the color wheel.

The original colors in the template reinforce the holiday theme of this ticket. In fact, green and red are almost exactly opposite each other on the color wheel, which makes them very close to true complementary colors.

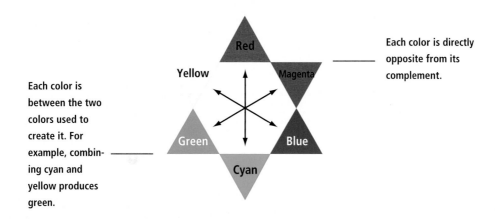

Each color is between the two colors used to create it. For example, combining cyan and yellow produces green.

Each color is directly opposite from its complement.

Tools:

Adobe PageMaker Plus
Adobe PhotoShop LE

Templates:

Certificates 1000502

Fonts:

(ITC) Giovanni,
(Adobe) Woodtype Orna-
ments, (ITC) Veljovic

Project 16

Adding Borders and Backgrounds to Certificates

Modify borders and create backgrounds for a distinguished award.

Customizing certificates is one area where you can let your imagination run wild. Since most certificates commemorate a personal or company achievement, you can use almost any font, background, or text color that reflects your business or the award being bestowed. Creating backgrounds in PhotoShop 5.0 LE and then adding them to your award adds a personal, unique touch.

Getting started. Open Certificates template 1000502. Save the template with a new name and turn off the Tips layer.

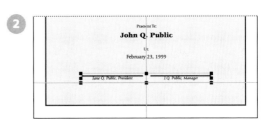

Delete and rearrange frames. In this example, we wanted to create a border all the way around the certificate and replace the current background. To accommodate the new border, we had to make room around the edges of the certificate.

To make room at the top, we used the pointer (⬆) to select and delete the overlapping decorative frames. To make room at the bottom, we deleted the company name and logo placeholders. If you want to keep the name and logo frames, drag them to a location nearer the center of the certificate.

To pull the President and Manager text frames in from the edges, we selected and grouped the text frames and the rules above them using the Elements > Group command. The frames were then resized and centered around the middle guide.

As a final step, we deleted the blue background.

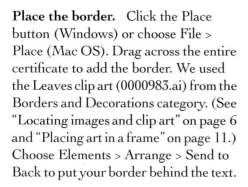

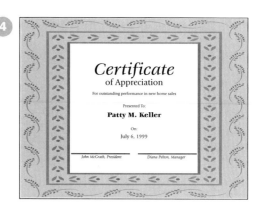

Place the border. Click the Place button (Windows) or choose File > Place (Mac OS). Drag across the entire certificate to add the border. We used the Leaves clip art (0000983.ai) from the Borders and Decorations category. (See "Locating images and clip art" on page 6 and "Placing art in a frame" on page 11.) Choose Elements > Arrange > Send to Back to put your border behind the text.

Replace the text. Select the text tool (**T**) and select and delete the placeholder text. Enter your own text.

Save your certificate. Just like that, your custom certificate is ready. Click the Save button () in the toolbar (Windows) or choose File > Save (Mac OS). Be sure to set your printer Orientation setting to Landscape before printing the certificate.

Variation: Create a textured background

There is an infinite variety of backgrounds you can use for certificates. The only limitation is that the background not overwhelm the text. In this example, we used the Clouds filter in Photoshop 5.0 LE to create a textured background.

Note the dimensions of the background. Use the pointer to select the certificate background. In the Control palette, note the height and width of the frame.

2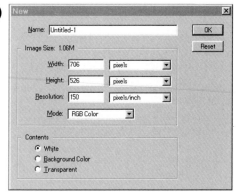

Create a Photoshop file. Click the Photoshop button () in the toolbar (Windows) or open the Photoshop LE application (Mac OS). Choose File > New and enter the dimensions you copied from the PageMaker file. Set the resolution to 150 and click OK.

3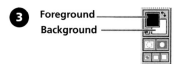

Change the foreground color. In the Photoshop toolbox, notice the two color swatches. These swatches indicate the foreground and background colors (they are black and white by default).

The Clouds filter (the filter we're using to create the texture) mixes the foreground and background colors to make a pattern. Click the foreground color swatch and select a new foreground color. Leave the background white or click and select a background color. Use pastel colors so that the background will not be too dark.

④

Apply the filter. Choose Filter > Render > Clouds. Soft clouds appear in the image.

⑤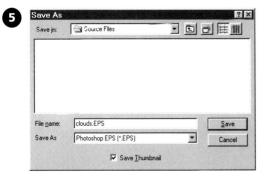

Save the file. Choose File > Save a Copy. In the dialog box, select Photoshop EPS in the Format menu and name your file. Click Save.

⑥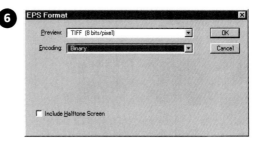

Accept the EPS settings. Click OK to accept the default settings in the EPS Format dialog box.

⑦ **Place the background in your certificate.** Return to PageMaker Plus Certificate template. Use the pointer to select the background frame and delete the blue background (if you have not already done so).

Choose File > Place and select your EPS file. Choose Element > Arrange > Send to Back to move the texture behind the text.

If you're going to be printing your certificate in black and white, try using one of the Photoshop filters, such as Chalk and Charcoal, that removes color from the image.

You may want to use a specific image as a background, but find that the image is too dark or clashes with the text and other graphics in the publication. You can lighten an image in Photoshop LE by decreasing its opacity, and then use the lighter image as a background.

The image you choose should be an RGB image, at least as large as the frame you're replacing. Choose a file with an image resolution of at least 150 dpi. (To find the size and resolution of an image, open the file in Photoshop LE and choose Image > Image Size.)

Do not attempt to increase the file dimensions or resolution in Photoshop or the image may appear blurry and degraded when you print the certificate.

1 In the certificate, select the background and note its dimensions in the Control palette. You need to use an image that is at least this large.

2 Open an image in Photoshop LE.

3 If the Layers palette is not showing, choose Window > Show Layers.

4 Double-click the Background layer and rename the layer. Click OK. (You can't change the opacity of a Background layer.)

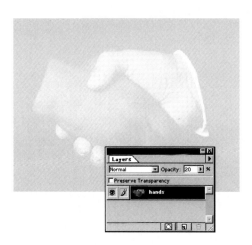

5 Select the renamed layer and drag the opacity slider in the Layers palette to about 20% or until the image is light enough so that it won't distract from the certificate text.

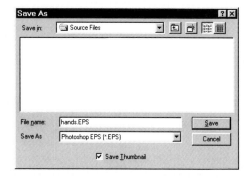

6 Save the file in Photoshop EPS format and place it in the PageMaker file.

Tools:

Adobe PageMaker Plus
Adobe Photoshop LE

Templates:

Postcards 2000641

Fonts:

AGaramond

Project 17

Creating Textures
for Postcards

Spice up your postcards with borders and textures.

12 Perk Rd., Bean,
WI 12345
Tel: 800 555 5515
Fax: 800 555 5516
info@coffee123.com
www.coffee123.com

Linda Lew

123 Mocha Court
Bean, WI 1234

Grand Opening!

Cafe Caruso is pleased to announce the opening of our second location. We will be open for business on September 2, 1999.

Free Cappuccino!

Join the grand opening fun! Bring this postcard and receive one free delicious cappuccino.

Postcards are one of the least expensive ways to spread your marketing message. Because of their small size, however, they can easily be overlooked in a stack of mail. Adding rules and textures can help your postcard stand out from the pack.

Getting started. Open Postcards template 2000641. Save the template with a new name and turn off the Tips layer. This is a two-page template, with a front and back.

Replace the text and logo. Use the pointer (➤) to select and delete the logo placeholder (the logo is made up of four separate squares). Replace it with your own logo. For more information on adding art to a template, see page 8.

Use the text tool (**T**) to select and replace the text in the return address section. You may want to delete the recipient address frame if you're using address labels for your postcards.

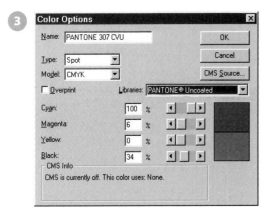

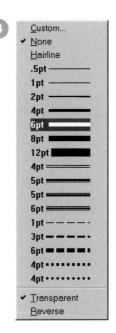

Add a new color. This template uses subtle, subdued colors. To grab a bit more attention, we decided to add more color. For detailed instructions on adding new colors to a template, see the design tip at the end of Project 9. We used Pantone 307 (a teal blue) from the Pantone Uncoated library.

Add a border. We decided to jazz up the postcard by drawing borders around the solid blocks of color already in the template. To add a border, select the frame and choose Element > Stroke and choose a width from the menu. We added a 6 point border to the box in the lower left corner of page 1.

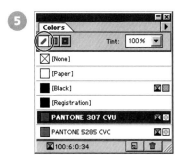

Change the stroke color. To add color to the border, make sure the border is selected. Click the stroke button (✎) in the Colors palette, and then click the color. We used our new color for the border.

Create additional borders. Click the 2 in the lower left corner to move to the second page of the template. Repeat steps 4 and 5 to add borders to one or more of the boxes on this page. To alter the effect slightly, try changing the color by choosing a new tint from the Tint menu in the Colors palette. (For more information on tints, see "Changing template colors" on page 14.)

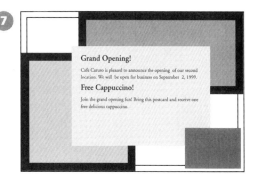

Replace the body text. Use the text tool to replace the placeholder headline and body text with your text.

This example adds a second headline. To match the style of the two headlines, we selected the second headline and clicked the MessageHead style in the Styles palette. We then selected the text and changed its color by clicking the new color in the Colors palette.

Save the postcard. Click the Save button (💾) (Windows) or choose File > Save (Mac OS) and you're ready to print your card. This template is designed to print with two spot colors. For more information on using spot colors see the input/output tip at the end of Project 19.

Variation: Adding texture with a bitmap file

Another way to add interest to a PageMaker template is to place a textured pattern in the template. It's easy to create a BMP bitmap file in Photoshop LE and then place it in the PageMaker publication. See the input/output tip at the end of this project for information on creating a bitmap texture file in Photoshop 5.0 LE.

Place the bitmap file. After we created a bitmap file that was as large as the postcard template, we selected the small box on page 1 of the template. We then placed the bitmap file (see "Placing art in a frame" on page 11). The pattern fills the box, creating a sense of texture.

②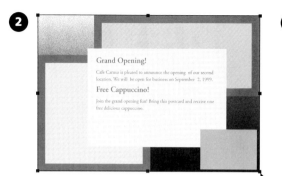

③

Send the pattern to the back. To add texture to the back of the postcard, we moved to page 2 and placed the bitmap image again. This time, we dragged the placement icon so that it filled the entire postcard. When we chose Element > Arrange > Send to Back, the pattern showed through all the lighter areas in the postcard.

Add color. To add color to the pattern, select the filled frame and click a color in the Colors palette.

The variation for this project shows you how to import a bitmap file and use it to create an interesting texture in your postcard. Here's how to create the bitmap file in Photoshop 5.0 LE.

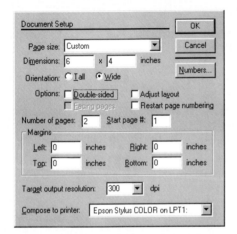

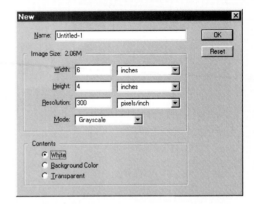

3   Choose File > New and enter the postcard dimensions. Set Resolution to 300 and choose Grayscale. (Don't choose Bitmap in the New dialog box or the gradient tool will not be available in your document.) Click OK.

1   In PageMaker, choose File > Document Setup and note the dimensions of the postcard template.

2   Click the Photoshop button () in the toolbar (Windows) or open Photoshop LE (Mac OS).

4   Make sure the foreground and background colors are set to their default black-and-white settings and select the gradient tool.

5 Press Shift as you draw a gradient from the bottom to the top of the image.

6 Choose Image > Mode > Bitmap.
Click OK to accept the default settings in the Bitmap dialog box. The gradient turns into a pattern.

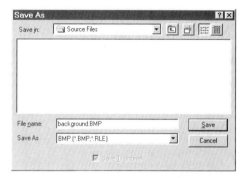

7 Choose File > Save a Copy and save in the BMP format.

8 In the BMP Options dialog box, select Windows file format and 1 bit depth.

9 Name your file Background. bmp and save it as a BMP file. You're ready to place the file in your PageMaker publication.

Tools:
Adobe PageMaker Plus

Templates:
Label Sets 1000787

Fonts:
Arial

Project 18

Using Imported Art in Labels

Create fun black and white name tags using a TIFF file.

You can use many types of graphics files in a PageMaker publication. The clip art on the PageMaker CD-ROM is in Adobe Illustrator (.ai) format. The images on the CD are in JPEG format. You can also use files in the Encapsulated Postscript (EPS), TIFF, GIF, and Kodak Photo CD formats, among others. (For a complete list, see the *Adobe PageMaker Plus User Guide*.)

This projects places a TIFF file in a black-and-white label. Since labels are something you use very often, keeping them simple and inexpensive can be a real time and money saver. These labels can be used as either address labels or name tags.

Getting started. Open Label Sets template 1000787. Save the template with a new name and turn off the Tips layer.

Zoom in on a label. In this template, the labels are laid out two across and five down. Choose View > Zoom in or drag around one label with the Zoom tool (🔍) to work on a single label.

Delete the logo. Use the pointer (🡤) to select and then delete each of the four boxes individually in the logo placeholder. Add your logo (see "Adding art to templates" on page 8). In this example, we will create a text logo for the label later in the project.

Add art. To dress up the label, we added a piece of art to the template. The art is a grayscale TIFF file that was added to the left of the rule. In general, TIFF and EPS files do best for low-resolution printing.

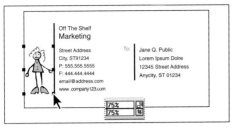

Scale the clip art. In most cases, the art you add will be too large for a template as small as this label. To resize this art, we selected it, entered 75% in the horizontal and vertical percent scaling options in the Control palette, and pressed Return. We then dragged the art so that the bottom edge lined up with the bottom of the vertical rule.

Create the name logo. Next, we added the company logo (which is text in our example). Using the text tool (**T**), we clicked above the art and typed Kid Art. In keeping with the children's theme, we used 12 point Kaufmann Bold font with 14 point leading. Since this is a single line of text, we chose the settings from the Control palette instead of creating a new style or modifying an existing style.

Rotate and position the text. To maintain the vertical design of this template, we decided to rotate the text before we positioned it above the art. With the text selected, we entered 90 in the Rotating option in the Control palette and pressed Return. Use the pointer if you need to adjust the position of the rotated text.

Replace the address text. Select and replace the address information (and the recipient information if you're using this as a mailing label). We added a marketing message to the frame that originally held the company name.

For information on the easiest way to duplicate the changes to the other labels in the template, see Project 2.

Save and print the labels. Click the Save button (🖫) in the toolbar (Windows) or choose File > Save (Mac OS). There are many Avery label stocks to choose from. See the complete listing of SKU numbers in the template information box.

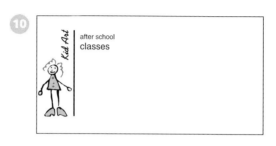

Turn the shipping label into a name tag. To use this label as a name tag, simply delete the To and Address text frames. Print the labels and then write in the names by hand.

Variations: Adding special effects to TIFF files

You don't need to go into Photoshop LE to add special effects to your art. You can create many cool effects right in PageMaker Plus when you're using imported TIFF files. To experiment with some different looks, place your black-and-white or color (RGB only) TIFF file in a PageMaker publication. Select the art and choose Element > Image > Photoshop Effects. From there, you're on your own!

Sprayed strokes

Note paper

Bas relief

DESIGN TIP: Choosing a font

Font styles can go a long way in conveying your company's image or the specific mood of a publication. Here are a few of the fonts shipped with PageMaker Plus and an indication of the moods they might evoke.

Practical

Frutiger
Myriad
News Gothic

Headlines

Blackoak
MACHINE
VAG Rounded

Formal

COPPERPLATE
Park Avenue
TRAJAN

Fun

ITC Kabel
Isabella
Willow

Technical

Letter Gothic
ORATOR
Serpentine

Traditional

Times
Bodoni
Goudy

Tools:
Adobe PageMaker Plus

Templates:
Signs 0000465

Fonts:
*American Typewriter,
Birch, Madrone*

Project 19

Spacing Text in Signs

Use kerning and tracking to fine-tune text.

Most of the time, the type characteristics in a template, including font, size, kerning, leading, and tracking, will fit your needs just fine. In some instances, however, especially when you add significantly more or less text to a frame, the type becomes difficult to read. To keep the professional touch in your publications, you can easily adjust the type characteristics.

Getting started. Open the Signs template 0000465. Save the template with a new name and turn off the Tips layer.

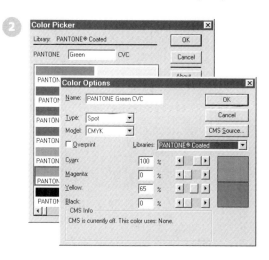

Replace a color. In this example, we used the shape of the art placeholder as a background for two pieces of clip art. First, we used the text tool (**T**) to select the Place Artwork Here text and deleted it.

We wanted the art frame and the text frame to be the same fill color, so we decided to change the red color to a

deep green. To replace a color, double-click the color in the Colors palette to display the Color Options dialog box, then choose a color library.

Choose the new color. In the color picker, choose the new color. We used Pantone Green CVC from the Pantone Coated library.

Change the tint. Replacing the red with green automatically changed the color of the For Sale frame. When you replace a color in the Colors palette, all the areas of the original color are replaced with the new color.

To change the placeholder fill, we used the pointer (▶) to select the frame, then clicked the new color in the Colors palette. The placeholder turned a light green, because it has a tint applied to it. We chose 100% from the Tint menu on the Colors palette to make both the frames the same intensity. The empty, colored placeholder was now ready to be used as a container for new art.

Place the art. Click the Place button (▣) in the toolbar (Windows) or choose File > Place (Mac OS) to place the art you want to use in the colored frame (see page 11). This example uses two gardening images (0001710.ai and 0001755.ai) from the At Home category. For information on locating clip art, see page 6.

Use the pointer to drag the art into position. We resized the art to make it slightly bigger. To place one image behind or in front of another, select the art and choose Element > Send Backward or Element > Bring Forward.

6

7

Replace the text in the bottom frame. Use the text tool (**T**) to replace the $1000 text. We typed Gardening Tools. Because the text is longer than the original, part of the text disappeared as we typed. We used the pointer to drag a handle to make the frame wider. As we resized the frame, the rest of the text appeared (Windows).

In the Mac OS, select the pointer and increase the frame width before you begin typing to accommodate longer text.

Reduce tracking. Tracking adds or deletes space between letters and words. When you add more or less text to a frame and want to maintain the frame's original size, you can change the tracking to expand or contract the text.

Because we increased the amount of text in the frame, we needed to reduce the tracking so that the text took up less space. To change tracking, select the text and click the tracking option (⯆⯆⯆) in the Control palette. We selected Very Tight from the menu to pull the letters and words closer together.

Increase tracking. Replace the text in the diagonal text box. We typed Save 30% on the first line and While Supplies Last! on the second line. Because this is less type than was in the frame, we needed to add more space between letters. We selected the text and choose Very Loose from the tracking menu to spread out the letters and words.

Apply kerning. Kerning determines the space between individual letters in a word. When you increase the size of

some type, the letters do not space evenly. You can manually adjust the spacing between these letters.

The word Sale contains irregular spaces between the characters. With the text tool selected, we placed the insertion point between the letters l and e. We then typed -.09 into the kerning option (⟨⟩) in the Control palette to replace the letters.

As a final touch, we replaced the word For with Tool.

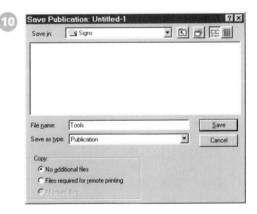

Save the sign. Click the Save button (🖫) in the toolbar (Windows) or choose File > Save (Mac OS). This sign prints on an 8.5x11 inch sheet of paper. For a thicker, more durable sign, consider printing it on card stock.

Variation: Enlarging a single letter

To create an eye-catching effect, try changing the characteristics of just one letter in a word.

Sizing and kerning. Use the text tool to select the first letter in a word (we selected the T in Tools). Make the letter larger using the size menu in the Control palette. Then use the pointer to select the frame and drag until you can see the new, larger letter.

Apply kerning. Place the text insertion point between the enlarged letter and the next letter in the word. Adjust the kerning by entering a value in the kerning option (⚏) in the Control palette (we entered –0.12). The adjoining letter is pulled closer to the first letter.

DESIGN TIP: Creating your own template

The dimensions of this sign template, meant to be printed on an 8.5- by 11- inch stock, would fit well in a store window or on a bulletin board. You can use this same design in a smaller version as a shelf-talker. Shelf-talkers are signs used as point-of-purchase advertisements. They hang down from the shelf directly above or below the product. This template can be easily modified to create a shelf-talker template.

1 Open your final Sign document, choose File > Save As, and give it with a new name. Choose Template from the Save as Type menu (Windows) or click Template under the Save As options (Mac OS). Click Save.

2 Choose File > Document Setup and change the orientation to Tall and the bottom margin to .5.

3 Drag a guideline down to the 5 inch marker in the vertical ruler to indicate where the fold line will be. The top half of the template will be blank so it can be inserted into the shelf above the product.

4 Choose Edit > Select All and then choose Element > Group to group all the objects.

5 Shift-click a corner handle and resize the grouped object until it fits in the bottom half of the page. Drag the art down.

6 Choose Element > Ungroup to separate the objects. Reposition the objects if needed.Resize the upper text box so that it fits above the triangle

7 Use the text tool to select the Tool and Sale text and apply the Price style from the Styles palette or choose a new font and size. (For more on applying styles to text, see see "Changing text styles" on page 13.).

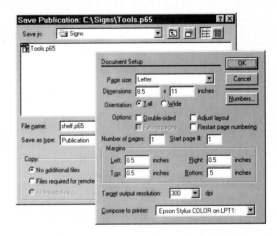

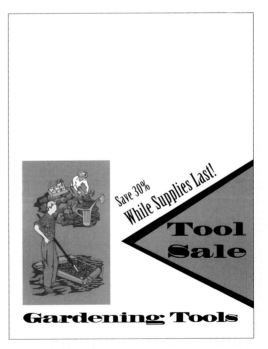

Spot color is used to print solid, flat areas on a printing press. The colors are chosen from a wide variety of premixed inks. Each spot color is reproduced using a single printing plate.

The Sign template in this project uses a single spot color. (In the Colors palette, a spot color is represented by the ⦿ icon.) A spot color printed at 100% is a solid color. If the color is lightened, it is printed as a *tint*. This is also called *screening* the color. Avoid using tints for small type or hairlines because they often appear as broken lines. Instead, use a single, solid color ink for rules and small text.

Because printing spot color requires only one ink (as opposed to the cyan, yellow, magenta, and black ink needed to print process colors), it is less expensive than full-color printing.

Use spot colors when you need three or fewer colors and you will not be using photographs in your publication. Spot color is also useful when you want the limited colors you get from one or two spot colors and their tints or when you need to match precisely the color used in your logo or other company graphics.

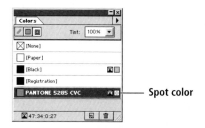

— **Spot color**

Tools:

Adobe PageMaker Plus

Templates:

Cards 1000615

Fonts:

Baker Signet

Project 20

Creating Unique Holiday Cards

Flip and skew text for special occasion cards.

Holiday cards are a perfect opportunity to expand your artistic horizons. Applying effects to images and text presents unlimited opportunities for creative expression. In this project, flipping and rotating the text produces an interesting cross between shadowed and mirrored text.

Getting started. Open Cards template 1000615. Save the template with a new name and turn off the Tips layer.

Edit the text on page 1. Shadow type works best when you apply it to a limited number of capitalized words. Use the text tool (**T**) to select and edit the text your want to use in your card (see "Replacing text" on page 12). To capitalize the text, click the all caps case button (C) in the Control palette.

In this example, we deleted and a Happy New Year! and changed Merry Christmas to all caps. The capitalization forced the text to two lines. To return to a single line, we reduced the font size to 24 point using the menu in the Control palette.

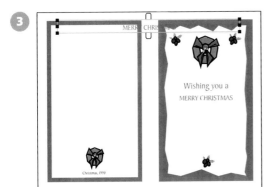

Copy and paste the text. Before you can flip it, you need to duplicate the text. Select the text and choose Edit > Copy. Switch to the pointer tool (⬆) and choose Edit > Paste. A copy of the text appears in its own text box at the top of the page.

We duplicated the Merry Christmas text.

Note: If you don't see the new text, you probably pasted it with the text tool still selected. If so, the text was pasted right on top of itself.

Position the text and change its color. Use the pointer to drag the copied text down, until it's directly under the original text. Select the copied text with the text tool and click Black in the Color palette. Change the tint to 30% to produce the shadow effect.

Flip the type. Switch to the pointer again and select the text box (the four black handles will appear). Click the vertical-reflecting button (F·Ł) in the Control palette.

Drag the flipped type so that the bottom edge abuts the original type. Drag guides from the vertical ruler to help you line up the edges of the text. You can use the arrow keys on your keyboard to nudge the text into position.

Skew the type. With the text box still selected, type -30° in the skewing option (⍁) in the Control palette (you may need to resize the text box). Drag until the copied text is lined up with the original text to produce the offset effect.

(7)

and a
Happy New Year
from
THE SULLIVAN TWINS

Variation: Flip images

You can also use the vertical-reflecting and flip effects on images. In this example, the image was flipped to produce mirror images.

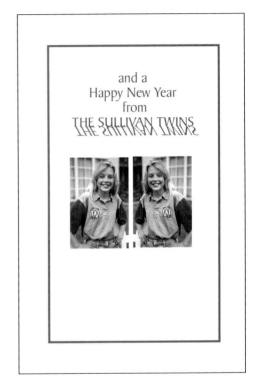

and a
Happy New Year
from
THE SULLIVAN TWINS

Edit and manipulate the text on page 2. Delete the text you will not use. Follow Steps 3 to 6 to alter the text on the inside of the card (even your name!). Shadow text doesn't need to be gray; try experimenting with other colors and tints.

(8) **Save your holiday card.** Click the Save button (🖫) in the toolbar (Windows) or choose File > Save (Mac OS). This card is designed to print on Avery stock SKU #8316.

You can customize the Pictures palette so that it contains the photos you use most frequently. You can even create new categories to group your photos in easy-to-remember libraries. For example, you may want to create a category for photos of your company products or a category for employee photos. After you've scanned in your photos or have had them stored on floppy disks, you can copy them to the Pictures palette.

Adding photos to the Pictures palette (Windows only)

1 Choose New Category from the Pictures palette menu.

2 Name the category and click OK.

3 Choose Add Photos from the Pictures palette menu. Navigate to the image you want to add and click Open. The image appears in the Pictures palette.

If you decide you'd rather move the photo to an existing category or store a copy in a second category, select the image and choose Move Pictures To (or Copy Pictures To) from the Pictures palette menu. Choose a category from the list.

Tools:

Adobe PageMaker Plus
Adobe Photoshop LE

Templates:

Programs 1000516

Fonts:

Bell Gothic, Bodoni,
Kaufmann, Woodtype
Ornaments

Project 21

Framing Photos for Programs

Use the Keyline plug-in to make your photos stand out.

PageMaker 6.5 Plus comes with several built-in plug-ins. (A plug-in is a small application that adds features to a program.) These plug-ins, which include graphic and text formatting aids, are found in the Utilities menu. In this project, we use the Keyline plug-in. A keyline is a thin line that surrounds an object or image and helps it stand out from the page.

Getting started. Open Programs template 1000516. Save the template with a new name and turn off the Tips layer. This is a two-page template that you fold in half to create the program.

Replace the art. Click the 2 in the lower left corner of the template to move to the second page. The second page contains the inside pages of the program.

Use the pointer (▸) to select the frame, then place your art (see page 11). Repeat this step for each photo place-holder.

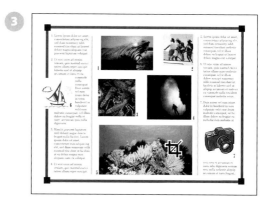

Adjust the art. If your images don't fit inside the frames, use the pointer (▸) to select the frame and resize the art. (For more information, see "Resizing art" on page 10 and "Repositioning and resizing art in a frame" on page 12).

4 **Replace the text.** Use the text tool (**T**) to select and replace the text on the inside pages. Each of the numbered paragraphs describes the photo of the same number.

6

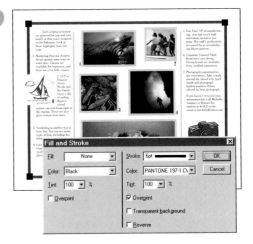

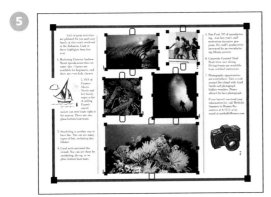

5

Add a keyline. Select the pointer and hold down Shift as you select the photos you want to have a keyline.

Define the keyline style. Choose Utilities > Plug-ins > Keyline. The number in the dialog box indicates how far the outside edge of the keyline extends from the image's boundary. We left this setting at the default value of .25 points. Click Attributes.

Choose a value from the Stroke menu and a color from the Color menu. In this example, the stroke is set to 6 and the color is set to Pantone 197 with a 100% tint.

Click Overprint. (Overprint fills the keyline shape with the paper color so any background color below the image is knocked out.) The images are outlined with a colored border.

7 **Add text and art to page 1.** Click the 1 in the lower left corner of the template to move to the first page. Use the text tool to replace the text in the two text frames.

Shift-click, using the pointer to select the symbol and circle placeholder art, then delete it. Add your own art (see "Adding art to templates" on page 8). This example uses the Scuba Diver image (0004683.jpg) from the Sports and Fitness category.

8

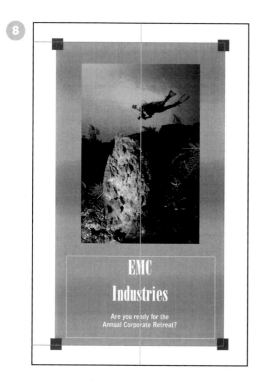

Position the graphic. Drag a vertical guide so that it divides the page. Drag the text down so that the photo does not cover the text. Use the guide to center the text and the photo.

9

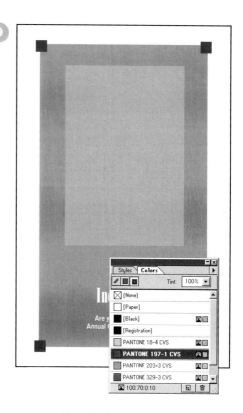

Create the shadow. As a final touch, we wanted to add a shadow effect around the opening graphic. To add a shadow, select the rectangle tool (□) in the toolbox and draw a rectangle that is the same size as the image and directly on top of it. Click a color in the Colors palette (or create a new color) to fill the rectangle (it will block out the photo). We used Pantone 197 for our fill color.

Offset the shadow. With the rectangle still selected, choose Element > Arrange > Send Backward. This moves the rectangle behind the photo.

Use the arrow keys on the keyboard to offset the rectangle from the image and produce the shadow effect.

11 **Save and print the program.** For a program with this many colored photos, you may want to have a professional printer do the job. The information box (see page 6) indicates that this template can be printed using four process colors and is intended to be printed on an 8.5x11 inch stock.

Variation: Create different keyline styles

Explore the choices available for filling and stroking with a keyline by experimenting with the settings in the Keylines dialog box. Select a photo, choose Utilities > Plug-ins > Keyline, and go to town.

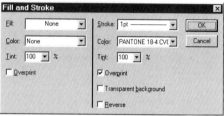

Single rule. This example uses a 1 point rule and Pantone 18-4 for a more subtle effect.

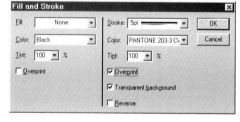

Double rule. This photo uses a 5 point double rule and Pantone 203-3.

A soft shadow adds a dreamy quality to images and helps them blend into the background. It's easy to create soft shadows in Photoshop LE.

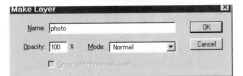

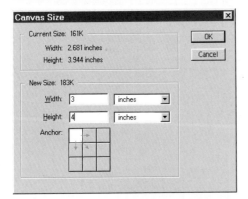

1   Open Photoshop LE and open the image file. Opened images appear on the Background layer.

2   Double-click the Background layer in the Layers palette to change it to a standard layer and name the layer "photo." (You can't change the position of a Background layer in the Layers palette.)

3   Choose Image > Canvas Size. Increase the width and height so you have room to add the shadow. Click the upper left Anchor box to add the new canvas to the right and bottom of the image.

4   Create a new layer for your shadow. Click on the top right triangle in the layers palette, and select New Layer. Name the new layer "shadow."

5   Drag the shadow layer below the photo layer in the Layers palette.

6   Press the control button (Windows) or the Command key (Mac OS) and click the photo layer (not the highlighted shadow layer) to select the image. A marquee appears around the image in the photo layer.

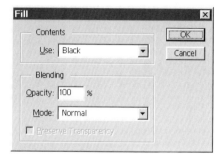

7 Choose Edit > Fill and choose Black from the Use menu. Leave Opacity set to 100% and Mode set to Normal.

8 With the shadow layer still highlighted, use the rectangular marquee tool ([ ]) to drag the selection marquee down and to the right, or wherever you want the shadow to be.

9 Choose Selection > Feather > and enter a feather radius of 10. Notice that the selection marquee now has rounded edges. The marquee indicates where the feathering will occur.

10 Choose Select > None.

11 Drag the opacity slider to lower the opacity to 50%.

12 Choose Save > Save a Copy and choose Photoshop EPS from the Format menu. You can then place the EPS file in your PageMaker Plus document.

Tools:
Adobe PageMaker Plus

Templates:
Cards 1000621

Fonts:
AGaramond, Kaufmann

Project 22

Enlivening Invitations with Inline Graphics

Use inline graphics to break up text.

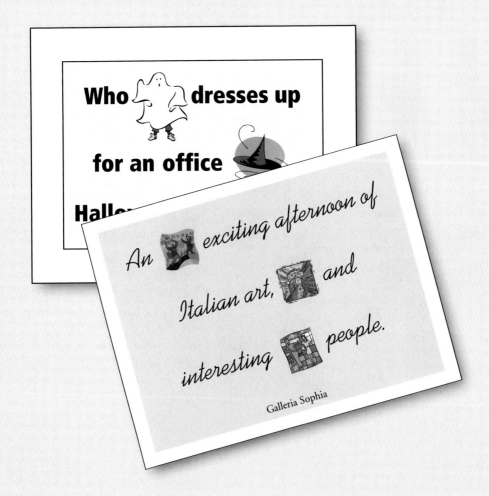

To make layout as easy as possible, the PageMaker 6.5 Plus templates create separate frames for text and graphics. This allows you to move and resize elements easily.

In addition to free-floating text and graphics, you can also attach a graphic to text. These graphics are called inline graphics. Since they are connected to the text, they move as you enter and delete text in a paragraph. This project uses inline graphics to add some fun to an invitation.

Getting started. Open Cards template 1000621. Save the template with a new name and turn off the Tips layer.

This template is designed to be printed on an 8.5x11 inch paper and then folded into quarters to make the invitation. When you're using a template that contains upside-down text, you can rotate the text frame, enter your text, and then rotate the frame back to its original position. This makes it much easier to enter and edit the text.

Place and rotate the logo. Start working in the upper right quadrant. Drag guides from the rulers to mark the bottom and center of the logo place-holder (see Project 2 for more on using guides). Use the pointer (⬆) to select the logo placeholder, then delete it and add your own logo (see "Adding art to templates" on page 8). Center the logo using the guides.

Select your logo and click the center dot in the Proxy (⊞) in the Control palette to set the rotation around the center point. Type 180 in the rotating option(◯) in the Control palette and click the Apply button (the button to the far left). The logo is turned upside down.

3

Edit the invitation text. Use the pointer to select the text frame above the logo and click the center dot in the Proxy (⊞) in the Control palette to set the rotation around the center point. Enter 0 in the rotating option and click the Apply button. The frame rotates on its top right corner. Type in your information. Select the frame with the pointer and type 180 in the rotating option. Click the Apply button, and the frame returns to its original orientation.

Scroll to the upper left quadrant of the template. Use this same method to replace the text in these frames.

4

Place art and edit the caption. Scroll to the lower left quadrant, delete the art placeholder, and add your own art. In this example, we used the Coliseum image (0001431.ai) from the Travel and Destinations category. Select the art and enter 180 in the rotating option (↻) in the Control palette to turn the image upside down. Click the Apply button. Drag the art into position.

Follow the directions in Step 3 to rotate, replace text, and return the caption text frame to its original location.

5

6 **Type the text.** Use the text tool to add your own text. Don't worry about line breaks because they will change when you add the graphics. This example uses "An exciting afternoon of Italian art and interesting people" as its text.

Resize the cover text frame. Scroll to the lower right quadrant. We used the pointer to select and drag the company name to the bottom of the page to allow more space for the invitation text.

We then selected and deleted the border around the large text frame. Removing the border allowed us even more room to increase the size of the text frame. We resized the frame, leaving about 1/4 inch around the top and sides of the page.

7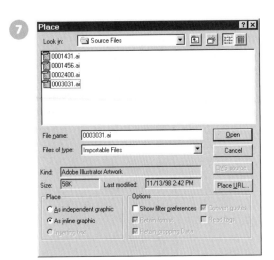

8

An ✦ exciting afternoon of
Italian art, ✦ and
interesting ✦ people.

Galleria Sophia

Place the inline graphics. Place the text insertion point where you want the first graphic to be placed (in this example, the insertion point is after the first word).

Click the Place button (▣) in the toolbar (Windows) or choose File > Place (Mac OS) and select the art you want to add. Make sure the As an Inline Graphic option is selected in the Place dialog box, and click OK. The first inline graphic in this example is the Celebration image (0003031.ai) from the Special Occasions category.

Adjust the size of the art. Since our art was too big for the design, we used the pointer to select the art. We then entered 30% in the Width and Height percentages boxes in the Control palette to reduce its dimensions. We used the text tool to click the insertion point before the graphic and added spaces to provide extra room around the art.

Repeat Steps 7 and 8 to place other inline graphics in the text. This example placed the Grand Canal image (0001456.ai) from the Travel and Destinations between the words art and and, and the Celebration image (0002400.ai) from the Special Occasion folder after the word interesting.

9

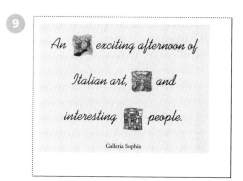

Galleria Sophia

Adjust line breaks and leading. Place the insertion point in the text where you want the text to break and hold down Shift as you press Enter (Windows) or Return (Mac OS).

To increase the spacing between the lines of text, you can change its leading (see Project 19). We entered 70 in the leading option (⫯ᴬ) in the Control palette. This opened the text so that there was plenty of space for the inline graphics.

10 **Save and print the invitation.** Click the Save button (🖫) in the toolbar (Windows) or choose File > Save (Mac OS). To make printing easier, you can take this invitation to your printer and request that it be printed on Avery stock SKU# 8315 (or get some of this stock yourself). This Avery stock is set up to print quarter-fold cards. If you'd rather, you can print the invitation on your own paper and fold it into quarters.

Variation: Manipulating inline graphics

Inline graphics, like any other graphics, can be manipulated once they are in the text. You can resize, rotate, skew, and change their alignment, but you can't apply other text characteristics, such as font or style, to a graphic. For an extra flare, try rotating the inline graphics in your invitation.

Galleria Sophia

Rotating inline graphics. Use the pointer to select the inline graphic and type 7 in the rotating option (↺) in the Control palette. Select another graphic and type -7 in the rotating option.

For information on adjusting the baseline position of inline graphics, see the *Adobe PageMaker 6.5 Plus User Guide*.

PageMaker Plus makes it easy for you to prepare your publications for a service provider. When you bring a file in to be printed, be sure you have all the components, such as fonts and graphics, on your disk.

1   Choose File > Save and save your file.

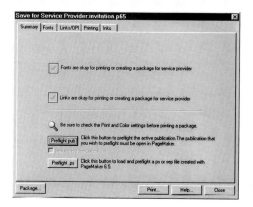

2   Choose Utilities > Plug-ins > Save for Service Provider. Click the Preflight Pub button. After a quick scan, two green checkmarks will appear. This tells you the publication is ready to go to the printer.

If you get an error message, you will need to correct the problem before proceeding. The message will tell you what needs to be done to prepare the file.

3   Once the green checkmarks appear, click the Package button in the lower left corner of the dialog box. The Package dialog box appears. Make sure the Include All Fonts (Windows) or Copy All Fonts (Mac OS) option is selected.
Note: Check that your service provider is licensed to use the fonts you are including. If not, you cannot copy or include the fonts.

4   Click Save. The computer will perform some checks for fonts and ink and then return you to the Save for Service Provider dialog box. Click Close.

Tools:

Adobe PageMaker Plus

Templates:

Cards 1000620

Fonts:

AGaramond

Project 23

Creating Elegant Quarter-Fold Cards

Use the Control palette to fine-tune text and graphics.

When you are fine-tuning your designs, the Control palette can be a real time-saving tool. This project uses the three views of the Control palette to make a lot of minor changes very quickly.

① **Getting started.** Open Cards template 1000620. Save the template with a new name and turn off the Tips layer. This template is designed to be printed on an 8.5 by 11 sheet of paper and then folded into quarters to make the card.

②

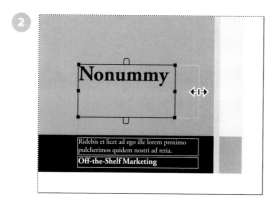

Resize the title frame. Scroll to the lower right quadrant of the card. To simplify the template design, we decided to make all the text frames on the cover the same size. To resize the frames, drag a guide from the vertical ruler to mark the right edge of the smaller text frames on the bottom of the cover. Use the pointer (⬏) to select the title text frame, then drag a handle to increase the frame width.

③

Replace the text. Use the text tool (**T**) to replace the text with your text. To add a touch of elegance to the card, we changed the type to small caps. To format text using small caps, select the text with the text tool and click the small case button (c) in the Control palette. The Control palette is currently in the character view. You use this view whenever you're making changes to character attributes, such as font, size, or leading.

Select and replace the text in the two bottom text frames.

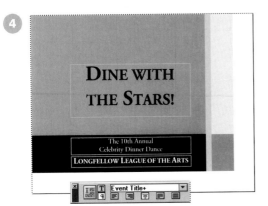

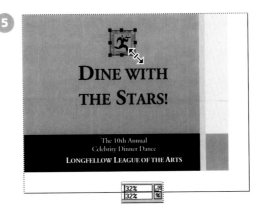

Change the paragraph alignment.
Click the insertion point anywhere in
the title text. Click the paragraph
symbol (¶) in the Control palette. The
options change, and you are now
viewing the Control palette in the
paragraph view. You use the paragraph
view to apply paragraph styles, change
alignments, and set other paragraph
attributes. We clicked the center
alignment button (≡) in the Control
palette to center the title text. We also
centered the text in the bottom text
frames.

Add a graphic. In keeping with the
redesign of this card, we decided to add
a graphic to the cover. You can add a
graphic anywhere in a template (see
page 8). This example uses the Waiter
image (0002727.ai) from the Food and
Dining category.

Note: *If you use the Place button (Windows)
or the File > Place command (Mac OS) to
add art, be sure the As New Item option is
selected in the Place dialog box. If you replace
a graphic in a frame, you won't be able to
move it freely.*

Use the pointer to select the graphic.
The Control palette changes to the
object view. In this view, you can
modify the size and orientation of the
selected object.

We wanted to make the graphic
smaller. To reduce a graphic, hold
down Shift as you drag a handle. The
values change in the width and height
percent scaling options. We reduced
this graphic until it was at 32% of its
original size. We then dragged the art
to the top of the cover.

6

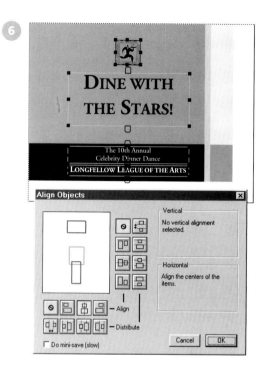

Align the elements. To keep the design consistent, we aligned all three text frames. To align objects, hold down Shift as you select the objects, then choose Element > Align Objects. We clicked the none option (⊘) for the vertical alignment and the center option (目) for the horizontal alignment.

7

Rotate the template. To make it easier to work on the text frames that are upside down in the template, you can rotate the entire template, make your changes, and then rotate it back into position.

Zoom out by pressing Control+ - (Windows) or Command + - (Mac OS) until you can see all the edges of the publication. Click the pointer and then drag around the entire template to select all the elements. Click the center dot in the proxy (⊞) in the Control palette to set the rotation around the center point. Type 180 in the rotating option in the Control palette. The entire template rotates. Choose Edit > Deselect All.

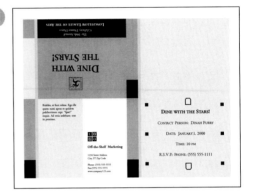

Delete placeholders. Scroll to the bottom right quadrant in the rotated template. Replace the art and text placeholders. In this example, we elected to remove these elements to make the template appear more spacious.

We then scrolled to the upper right quadrant and selected and deleted everything but the large text frame.

Replace the text. Because we wanted to leave the inside left quadrant empty, we dragged the text frame down to the bottom right quadrant. The frame was resized and made wider.

Use the text tool to select and replace the text with your own. Click the paragraph symbol (¶) in the Control palette and click an alignment button. We centered the text.

Click the character symbol (**T**) in the Control palette to format the text. We made the text small caps by clicking the small caps button (c) so that the text matched the text on the front of the card. To open up the text, we entered 36 in the leading option (↕) in the Control palette.(For more about leading, see Project 19.)

Add your logo and text to the back panel. Scroll to the left and select and replace the logo and text in the place-holders on the back panel.

Return the template to the printing position. With all your changes made, select the pointer and drag around the entire template. Click the center button in the proxy in the Control panel to set the rotation point and type 180 in the rotating option. The template reverts to its original layout. Choose Edit > Deselect All, and your elegant invitation is ready to go.

Save your publication. Click the Save button (▣) in the toolbar (Windows) or choose File > Save (Mac OS). Like the invitation in Project 22, this card is designed to print on Avery stock SKU #8315.

Variation: Add a graphic

To unify the invitation, you can add a graphic to the inside page where the contact information appears.

Use the pointer to select the graphic on the cover. Choose Edit > Copy. In the text frame on the inside page, add an extra Return where you want to place the graphic. Choose Edit > Paste. Enter 180 in the rotating option to turn the graphic right-side-up. Drag to center the graphic.

Variation: Add a color accent

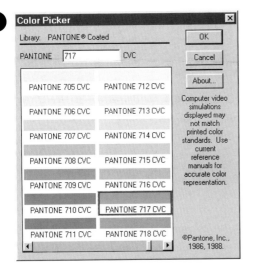

The graphic on the cover will stand out more if you add an accent color. Choose New Color from the Colors palette and choose Pantone Coated from the Libraries menu. Select a color (this example uses Pantone 717 CVC).

Select the vertical colored boxes that run the length of the invitation and click the orange color in the Colors palette (there are four boxes in all). Change the tint to 100% in the Colors palette.

As you become more familiar with PageMaker Plus 6.5, you'll probably feel more adventurous in your modification of the templates. The elements in a template serve to remind you of the types of information to include, but don't let them limit you. Nor should you feel you need to fill every text frame or place a graphic in every placeholder. Let your own sense of design guide you.

This Card template can lend itself to many different looks. In choosing to delete some items, rearrange others, and increase the leading, the template opens up and takes on a cleaner look appropriate to an elegant invitation. With other art and added elements, the card looks quite different.

Tools:

Adobe PageMaker Plus

Templates:

Ads 3000606

Fonts:

Bodoni

Project 24

Using Drop Caps in Advertisements

Include drop caps to add a design element to blocks of text.

Sometimes it's mandatory that you have large blocks of text in your publication. Whenever you have lots of text—in newsletters, brochures, reports, or scholarly ads—you can break up the monotony using drop caps. PageMaker Plus provides a plug-in that makes creating drop caps a snap.

1 **Getting started.** Open Ads template 3000606. Save the template with a new name and turn off the Tips layer.

2

Replace the text. Use the text tool (**T**) to enter your company name and address at the bottom of the ad.

Use the pointer (**↖**) to select and delete the headline frame and enter your own headline.

In this example, we're going to use two separate words instead of one long headline. We deleted the text frame and entered new text. Using the text tool, we placed the insertion point in the left column and typed "Then...". We then placed the insertion point in the right column and typed "Now". We selected each word and applied the Headline style from the Styles palette. To make the words very large, we changed the font size to 72 in the Control palette. Finally, we used the pointer (**↖**) to select the headline text boxes and drag them until they rested on the horizontal guide.

Use the text tool to select and then delete the body placeholder text. There are several ways to replace the body text:

• If you're entering original text, place the insertion point in the body text and choose Edit > Edit story. Enter your text in the story editor. When you've finished entering the text, choose Edit > Layout View to return to the publication. For more about the story editor, see Project 12.

• If you're using text from another source, use the pointer to select the text frame and choose Edit > Place. Make sure the Replacing entire story option is selected in the Place dialog box, then click OK.

Use autoflow. No matter how you get the text into the template, it will automatically flow from one column to the next. That is because these columns are *threaded*, that is, they are set up to make the text move from one frame into another.

Use the pointer (➤) to select the left text frame. Notice the plus sign in the bottom windowshade. The plus sign indicates that there is more text than can fit into this column. The remaining text automatically flows into the right frame.

In this example, a lot of text was added. Both columns were extended to the bottom of the page, and both are filled with text.

4

Replace the logo. Use the pointer to select and delete the logo placeholder and replace it with your logo. The logo used in this example is partially covered by the text. You can solve this problem by using text wrap to bump the type away from the logo. Select the logo and choose Element > Text Wrap. Click on the center wrap option, then click OK.

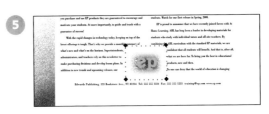

Adjust the wrap. To adjust the wrap, click on the points on the wrap boundary and drag until you have the shape you want. For more on using text wrap, see Project 8.

Replace the art. Use the pointer to select the art placeholder. Delete the placeholder and add your own art (see page 8 and page 11). After adding the art, we dragged it into the left column, until its left edge was up against the pattern in the left margin. We then used the pointer to resize the art until it touched the left center guide.

Add the art to the right column.

Add a colored shape. To add a background for our reverse text, we used the rectangle frame tool (⊠) to draw a rectangle under the photos. We then selected the frame, clicked the fill button in the Colors palette, and clicked Pantone 192-1 to fill the rectangle with blue.

8

Create reverse type. Click the Headline style in the Styles palette, then use the text tool to type in your text (in this example, We Have What You Need!). The black text on the blue background will be difficult to see. Select the text and click the reverse style button (⬛) in the Control palette to turn the text white. You may need to change the text size or tracking or increase the text frame width to make your text fit. This text is 48 point with a Tight tracking. (To find out more about tracking, see Project 19.)

9

Drop cap					✕
Drop cap			Go to paragraph		Close
Size: 3 lines	Apply	Remove	Prev	Next	

Create a drop cap. To break up the blocks of text, you can use drop caps. To create a drop cap, place the text insertion point in the first paragraph in the left column. Choose Utilities > Plug-ins > Drop Cap. We entered 3 in the lines box to set the height, then clicked Apply and Close. Choose a paragraph in the right column and apply another drop cap.

10

Add color to the drop caps. You can make the drop caps a different color by selecting the letter and clicking a color in the Colors palette. We turned the caps the same color blue as the rectangle frame. Select and apply the same color to the other drop cap.

11 **Save your advertisement.** Click the Save button (💾) in the toolbar (Windows) or choose File > Save (Mac OS). Many advertisers create PDF files to send to their printers. For more information on preparing a PDF file for the printer, see the input/output tip at the end of Project 7.

Color can be a confusing topic when you're preparing a file to go to a printer. Here are a few tips to keep in mind.

Offset printing uses one of two types of ink, process and spot. Process colors are reproduced by printing overlapping dots of cyan, magenta, yellow, and black to reproduce a large number of different colors. Since these inks are translucent, they absorb some colors and reflect others. To create blue, for example, you combine cyan dots and magenta dots. Your eyes merge the two colors to perceive the color blue.

Spot colors inks are printed with premixed inks, each specified to produce a different color. They are a solid color and have no dot pattern. For more on spot colors, see the input/output tip at the end of Project 19.

When you are creating a color in PageMaker Plus, or you want to know what type of inks are used in a particular template, check the Colors palette. The icons to the right of the colors identify whether they are spot or process colors.

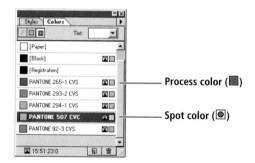

Process color (▣)

Spot color (◉)

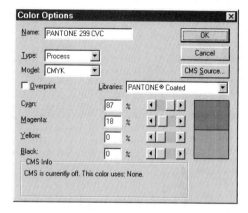

When you create a new color in PageMaker Plus, you have the option of making it a spot or process color.

When the template contains a photograph or color clip art, you print it with process colors. In general, you use process colors when:

○ You need more than three colors in your design. (Printing with process inks costs less than printing with three or more spot inks.)

○ You want to reproduce scanned color photographs or color artwork that can be reproduced only with process colors.

Some templates use a combination of spot and process colors. When you have both types of color in one template, extra plates are required for the spot colors. This can increase the price of your print job. Make sure you check with your printer before you decide what kind of ink to use.

Index

About the authors

Kate O'Day:

Kate O'Day has been a writer and photographer for over 20 years. Her company, Kate O'Day and Associates, has provided instructional design and technical documentation for numerous clients, including Adobe Systems, Apple Computers, Netscape Communications, Claris Corporation, and Macromedia. She has also authored books for Adobe Press, Hayden Books, and the Waite Group.

As a photographer, Kate has documented historical sites and ritual events around the San Francisco Bay Area. Recently, she has been photographing spiritual sites in Ireland. For more information about Kate O'Day and Associates and the Portraits of Ireland project, visit the www.koday.com website.

Linda Tapscott:

Linda Tapscott has been a graphic artist for 17 years. Her company, Spitting Image, has designed and produced projects for Adobe Systems, Microsoft, and *Apple International* magazine. Linda was responsible for designing and creating the illustrations for the *Adobe Photoshop 3.0 User Guide* and is the coauthor of *The Amazing PhotoDeluxe Book* and *Guerrilla Marketing with Adobe PhotoDeluxe Business Edition*.

Linda is also a contemporary artist who combines her technological skills and exploratory fine arts creativity. Her works have been exhibited in numerous shows and galleries around the San Francisco Bay Area. Linda's work can be seen on the Internet at www.ltapscott.com.

Dedication:

For Brendan and Alex, "The longest road out is the shortest road home." — Kate O'Day

For Bill, Michelle, Dinah and Shoei, "You keep me sane with laughter." — Linda Tapscott

Thanks to:

Kate Paddock (Project 18)

Barbara Scheer (Projects 8 and 21)

Michelle-Jean Waddell (Projects 1, 2, 3, 4, and 5)